Kenelm Henry Digby

Hours with the First Falling Leaves

Kenelm Henry Digby

Hours with the First Falling Leaves

ISBN/EAN: 9783742829146

Manufactured in Europe, USA, Canada, Australia, Japa

Cover: Foto ©Thomas Meinert / pixelio.de

Manufactured and distributed by brebook publishing software
(www.brebook.com)

Kenelm Henry Digby

Hours with the First Falling Leaves

8vo. cloth, price 10s. 6d.

THE VOIAGE AND TRAVAILE OF SIR JOHN MAUNDEVILE, Kt.

1322-46.

Which treateth of the way to Hierusalem ; and of the Marvayles of Inde, with other Ilands and Countryes.

Originally printed in English by RICHARD PYNSON. Now reprinted, with an Introduction, Notes, and a Glossary by J. O. HALLIWELL, Esq.

Illustrated with Seventy-two most curious Wood Engravings.

"The romantic and mythical element in our first Oriental traveller is what chiefly interests the modern reader, by its revelation of the feelings of an extinct world, and by the measure it supplies of the distance that the European mind has travelled in five centuries. But we should be doing the old wanderer a great injustice if we did not recognise the good sense with which he handles all that, from his point of view, fell under the cognizance of mere good sense. His accounts of the state of the East, as seen by himself, are valuable from their trustworthy sagacity."—*Pall Mall Gazette.*

"Wherever English, in its early, robust, manly form, is read, Sir John Maundevile is admired. His humble piety, his solemn reverence for the holy places which he visited, his simple faith in all he heard, his acute observation of what he actually saw, his self-sacrifice, his devotion, his credulity, his firm faith, his long endurance, appear in almost every page, and make his volume not only the earliest, but one of the noblest, of its class."

4to. sewed, price 2s. 6d.

OBSERVATIONS ON THE ORIGIN OF THE DIVISION OF MAN'S LIFE INTO STAGES. By J. WINTER JONES, Esq. Principal Librarian of the British Museum. Illustrated with a large folding plate, being a Fac-simile from an unique woodblock of the 15th century preserved in the British Museum ; also a Fac-simile from a Dutch Wood Engraving of the Ten Ages of Man.

Crown 8vo. cloth, price 12s. *Illustrated with Fifty Wood Engravings.*

A MANUAL OF METALLURGY, more particularly of the Precious Metals, including the Methods of Assaying them. By G. H. MAKINS, Esq. one of the Assayers of the Bank of England.

F. S. ELLIS,
33 KING STREET, COVENT GARDEN, LONDON.

HOURS WITH THE FIRST FALLING LEAVES.

BY

KENELM HENRY DIGBY, Esq.

AUTHOR OF

"THE BROADSTONE OF HONOUR," "MORES CATHOLICI," &c.

London:

F. S. ELLIS, 33, KING STREET, COVENT GARDEN.

1868.

LONDON:
GILBERT AND RIVINGTON, PRINTERS,
ST. JOHN'S SQUARE.

CONTENTS.

HOURS WITH THE FIRST FALLING LEAVES.

———•———

THE PRELUDE.

I SEEK not great things from the Muse,—
What others might with glory use;
I only ask that I may find
Some stranger of congenial mind,
Whom none perhaps can well define,
So truant all his thoughts, like mine,
So free from limits, outlines hard,
Which little would become a Bard,—
Who, like a painter, needs must dread
Harsh hues, unblended, coarsely spread,
Instead of gentle neutral tints,
As if no cries, but rather hints.
Then let me find this stranger bland,
Who thoughts like these will understand,
Although suspected by the crowd
For shouting nothing fierce aloud,—

That vulgar crowd which loves a glare
Shining through fog and frosty air.
Give me the man, who, like the light
Of day, tones down for human sight
All that he sees, and leaves the Hill
Cerulean, soft, and distant still,—
Who in a pleasant, sunny nook,
At some small leaves may deign to look,
Just as his eyes would quickly pass
From laurels to the daisied grass,
From sprigs that line the bright Alcove
To Doves alighting from their grove;
From Roses that perfume the air
To some slight weed that shelters there ;
From gorgeous clouds that float on high
To microscopic things that fly
Just far enough to reach their cell
Within some flower's purple bell.

Grand volumes suited to the crowd,
Of which great readers boast aloud,
Cannot, perhaps, for all dispense
With little books of no pretence ;
Which only will refuse to aid
Those who would turn our light to shade,
Renouncing all restraint's controls,
Though " Poets have the charge of souls [1] "—

[1] V. Hugo.

A martyr's glory to achieve
To utter truth and not deceive,
For times or men no fawning breath,
Preferring simply loss or death.
Your tomes of travels, which alone
Your clubs and booksellers will own,
Might surely leave a tiny space
For those which mental journeys trace—
For flights of soul above the crowd
Which few are found to praise aloud,
Although in speed, and not in vain,
They far surpass your boasted train,
Bearing the mind aloft to soar
Where dull, cold sorrow's felt no more.
Man, at this moment, it is said,
" Exists not by his heart and head,
But has a tendency to fall
Down into his intestines all."
I cite an Author of our age
Who for old manners shows no rage.
He says we should restore the reign
Of the best monarch, which is Brain.
He says the noblest Restoration
Is when the heart has domination.
He says the social question now,
What should engage man's earnest vow,
Is, more than ever, how to see
Revived the human dignity.
Immediate, urgent, is the need,
He says, for writers this to heed.

But sooth, when all is said and done,
I doubt if we shall see them run
To lend a hand thus to restore
What seems to perish more and more.
Still, thus impress'd, there are who try
To yield for some a small supply,
Just suited to the faint demand
Of what but few will understand.
And then for their own interest too
They ought to keep these tracks in view.
" 'Tis probable," says Cicero
(Whose mind no certainty could know),
" That if you leave what·best you can
To aid the future race of man,
Something there is of which the sense
You will possess when you are hence,
After your death, beyond this life
Of pain and error, tears and strife [2]."
The stream of Time may bear along
Like lightest leaf some simple song.
No words from any pen have pass'd
That may with time itself not last.
Let poets then from blame be free,
That they may serve posterity—
That so their hopes may have for rest
What even heathens knew was best—

---

[2] " Verisimile est, cum optimus quisque maxime posteritati
serviat, esse aliquid, cujus is post mortem sensum sit habi-
turus." (Tuscul. i. 15.)

Subordinate to our supply
Which makes so many wish to die.
Perhaps such leaves will float and pass
Unnoticed by the common mass,
Though even this is not so sure.
Attention trifles may secure ;
Like one pale leaf that drifted by,
Which made the passing maiden sigh.
Some say there lurks a charm most sweet
In books that but few readers meet.
Faint echoes of some distant sound,
Pale flowers in waning summer found,
Wild dreams that seem to soar and pass
As wakeful eyes regard the grass,
These, found in little books, belong
To men who shun emotions strong ;
Like butterflies of common kind
Whom connoisseurs disdain to find,
They please the simple in their Bower,
Who let them fly from leaf to flower.
May such a reader now be found
To hold my book and gaze around,
Not proudly, in a constant hurry,
As if he wish'd no rest, but flurry ;
Nought loving but excitement strong,
And that the better when it's wrong,
Sensational—his only test
Of what in letters he thinks best—
But one with leisure, thoughtful made,
Who can enjoy both sun and shade,

With that fine, exquisite, deep sense
Of things for which hard minds are
    dense—
Who has his fancies for retreat,
His favourite accustom'd seat;
Whom old familiar corners please,
As one who loves pure Nature's ease;
For these can bring back times gone by,
And so perennial joy supply.
As birds whose hearts are knit with home,
And far from it would never roam,
Such strangers often like to rest
Where once they found a sunny nest;
While others had through new scenes
    ranged,
They would prefer what is unchanged,
And so admire kind Nature's law
From which they true contentment draw;
For poorest urchins in the street
Find their accustom'd shelter sweet;
And highest Genius will confess
That habit yields delightfulness.
Thus I would have my audience free
From worshipping publicity;
One who can trust himself and judge,
Not always after others trudge;
In heart who condescends to herd
With one of whom he never heard,
Provided he is found to say
Things that will suit our common clay,

Our common heart, our common soul,
And never boast to know the whole,
To span which is refused to Pride,
When all its efforts have been tried.

The Muse herself may like to fly
Thus low at times, and shun the sky;
She can be careless like us all;
Though, when she leaves her azure hall,
Proceeding forth in gorgeous state,
There are who on her grandeur wait;
But even then she is content
When children are before her sent;
For greatness, when augustly shown,
Some nameless servants still must own.
Though first and smallest in her train,
Of me, perhaps, she won't complain.

THE TURN OF THE LEAF.

Oh! tell me, stranger, explain to me
What is this change that I feel and see?
The sky still so bright, the air serene;
Flowers still blooming, the grove so green.

Just as we saw them that pleasant day
When we would thoughtfully, sweetly stray
To the Muse's Hill's bright fairy slopes,—
The present a dream! with brighter hopes?

What, then, is changed in Nature around?
The breeze is soft, enamell'd the ground;
Still charms of Eden; and yet, and yet,
Something is gone that I can't forget!

Is it a perfume that floats in air?
Is it a colour in sunbeams there?
Is it in trees, in flowers, or grass?
In looks, or the steps of those who pass?

A change has arrived, I feel and see.
Tell me, oh! tell me, what can it be?
Exactly the same, I know not how,
Nothing is felt or experienced now.

Wait but a little; you soon will know
Why these sensations, why it is so;
Or if this instant some one must say,
Ask the astronomer what's the day.

September arrived, its twelfth sun past,
Could you expect the vision to last?
Summer that kindles, that lights the face,
Which in the heart with the sky keeps pace?

Excursions design'd, I fear, will prove
Somewhat congenial to plaintive love.
If you would all my prognostics know,
Sadness engender'd will with us go.

Yet, strange, ne'er heeding the printed page,
To find now thus alter'd Nature's stage.
Where is my warrant? what is my book?
It is that within, you mark and look.

It is that somehow your heart must feel
How Time unperceived will onwards steal.
A short space later, the winds will rise;
Leaves will be falling through darken'd skies.

Already, and prematurely all,
They flutter to sink, they soar to fall,
Fresh, like the youth that we loved the most,
Of hearts and Nature the pride and boast.

Poor tiny leaf, still so green, oh! how
Can you forsake thus your native bough?
The sun still willing to shine around—
And yet, forsooth, you sink to the ground!

Why should you heed how planets may roll,
You, such a wee small part of the whole?
Let the machine of the world all turn;
That is no reason you should inurn

Delicate foliage, with members fine,
Texture as wonderful just as mine.
Some more days pass'd; still the garden fair
Embalm'd with its breath the lightsome air.

But grey clouds gather'd, the winds did rise,
Movements of orbs took all by surprise.
The leaves, not as stragglers, few and lone,
Flutter'd in groups till the grass was strewn.

Trees seem'd to murmur a faint, wild sigh,
Grieving that changes far worse were nigh ;
Grass, flowers, groves, seem'd all to complain ;
The one thing joyous who would remain ?

Vaguely I felt the sadness around,
And caught from afar the plaintive sound.
'Tis said that the wind where palm-trees grow
Can scare with moans those who pass below.

Murmurs funereal create a tone
Of fear, and not of surprise alone.
Well, but mankind should still understand
More than leaves to escape and withstand

Changes that fluctuate all through life,
When grief and joy are ever at strife ;
Leaves are now falling, but even they
May have still something joyous to say.

In days of Autumn, when Nature dies,
We catch what's better than endless sighs ;
'Tis tender farewells, songs to the last,
However soon the whole must be past.

Perfumes to zephyrs are thrown from all
The drooping flowers with leaves that fall;
Through them the fast-cooling winds will bring
Melodies just like those heard in Spring.

'Tis poets, not leaves, that sadly moan,
Thinking they echo but Nature's tone;
E'en to leaves wither'd they should not dare
Their lamentations pale to compare.

For leaves will skip briskly, dance, and fly,
While poor Lamartine can only sigh.
Leaflets dismiss'd to wander alone
Have not caught always his dismal tone.

Butterflies, therefore, we still can see
Seeming to relish their company,
Clad in such colours, so varied fair,
Such as then every leaf will wear.

Faded leaves just as well as the new
Receive bright pearls of morning dew;
Contented, cheerful, they meet our eyes
With beauty that still can all surprise.

E'en in the wild storm when raging near—
Yes, even there, in the whirlwind's ear,
They seem still to whisper tales of mirth
As in the Spring which gladden'd the earth.

Still round you then on the grass is spread
A light of laughter from the bright bed
Of many a leaf although forlorn,
As you might think, from the others torn.

For leaves and flowers, e'en in decay,
Have somewhat cheering left still to say,
Like saintly age when it sinks to rest,
And all its words are yet bright and blest.

As when Lope de Vega in death,
While singing, exhaled his latest breath;
Like the Bard greater that Spain did own,
The holy, immortal, Calderon.

Such leaves will fall from the human tree,
Like those of the garden, sportive, free.
Mark how the latter are still array'd,
With no repulsive or gloomy shade;

Bright with the sun they skip on the grass,
Or bide in hairs of the passing lass.
Colour is changed; but playful and gay
They dance and pursue their downward way.

They twist and curl, and seem to demand
If a sweet laugh you can't understand.
Upwards they soar—for a moment—true;
Still they invite you the same to do.

Even descending to wormy bed,
They bid you lie down with placid head.
Scarlet, and yellow, and purple tints
They show, as so many silent hints

That we should bear lightly each thing sad,
Wing'd with such brightness as can be had ;
That nought should fret, discolour, surprise,
Those who reflect that no sparrow dies,

No hair can from auburn tresses fall,
Unnoticed by Him who loves us all.
Foliage preparing to leave us so,
Lessons right joyous can thus bestow.

Let it be still, then, the Muses' Hill,
Where gladness and thought may have their fill ;
We'll mount to the vast, the great, sublime ;
We'll skim quite low to a merry chime.

Rise with mists that have play'd on the ground,
Sink with vapours that highest were found.
High may be thoughts from which laughter
    springs ;
Low on thatch'd roofs rest the swallow's wings.

When a young giant, at Poictiers bred,
Saw the sad life that the scholars led,
Not knowing well how to pass their time,
He flung them a rock on which to climb,

In midst of a field where they might play,
On four great pillars placed where it lay,
On which they scramble and carve their names ;
And him for this fancy no one blames.

Why on my trifles should any spend
Wrath, since they answer the selfsame end?
Thanks to some pedagogues, coughers old,
Youths cease to be kind, merry, and bold ;

Grown fretful, dreamy, timid, and sly,
They can find no one to love them nigh.
Let them but take such nonsense in hand,
They become generous, peaceful, bland.

True, critics present, the safest thing
Would, sooth, be nothing like this to sing.
Coming at first to these walks so fair,
I wish superiors may not be there ;

As when on the Thames we seek our boat,
We want no grandeur with us to float ;
For when great judges are watching near,
Songsters or talkers must needs feel fear.

Till such men have left us and wander'd hence
No sound should escape our iv'ry fence.
" Till our superiors away are sped,
Silence is best," Epicharmus said[3].

[3] Athen. lib. viii.

But who can think that your critics sage
Will take in hand such an humble page?
Therefore I'm off with the bee to flowers,
Where I now seek my late summer bowers.

From two distinct chords, gravity, glee,
May spring up the sweetest harmony.
Joy in itself is religion pure;
As religion is joy, constant, sure.

All nature invites us thus to sing,
And plume for flight our soul's azure wing.
Leaves are our friends; but if they will fly,
To bear with their fall we needs must try.

To them it is true we owe a debt
Which those who lose them should not forget.
Some have assuaged the traveller's thirst,
Where from the ground no water would burst;

Others, protected from summer's rain,
Cheerful groups would around them maintain;
Others gave roofs for the peasant's cot,
All from the sun, a cool shelter'd spot;

Yet mark how the tree survives them all,
As year after year whole races fall.
Old oaks may have seen two thousand pass,
Moulder away in the common mass;

Then two thousand times beholding spread
Fresh generations that crown its head.
Leaves that I scatter may some be green ;
Others will glow with some sweet hue's sheen.

Minds should resemble the Orchidees,
Yielding fragrance to every breeze ;
Waning of seasons to them unknown,
Following each his fancy alone ;

Dreading no epochs, but ever free,
Yielding their perfume capriciously.
Some would have all things solemn and grave,
Thinking consistency thus to save.

As if e'en the woods had but one tone,
Never diversified, dark, alone.
But here expressly I'd mingle all,
Just as in Nature are great and small,

The palm'd consistency they esteem,
Thinking a partial and morbid dream.
Mirth and woe are befitting the soul
Of him who seeks to embrace the whole.

THE SUPERNATURAL.

O WOODLAND glades and depths, O gardens fair,
What signs, what traces, and what footsteps
    there!
What wonders in the vegetable reign,
If custom did not gratitude restrain!
Amazed we hear of trees producing bread,
Milk, water, wine, as is by travellers said;
But when our sylvan secrets have been told,
Our praise is scanty and our feeling cold;
And yet our woods disclose an art as high
As aught in tropic regions men descry.
The Druids would converse with the Divine
Where mystic light for them in oaks did shine.
In sycamores we oft are train'd to see
Zaccheus climbing on that wayside tree,
Where he so blest by faith would Christ behold—
The truth embodied that was long foretold;
Whose footsteps paved the ways of men with light
Which never endeth from the world's sight.   ·
The Lombard poplar still points to the skies
To lure us upwards when our spirit flies,
Gracing the groves like cities with a spire,
As if to make us heaven the most admire.
The willow, by kind Providence aye placed
Amidst the wet and fever-breeding waste,

Proclaims a hodiernal mystery
Of God for man supplying remedy,
Adjustment compensating for disease,
By granting what can cure, and thereby please,
According to a gracious wide-spread law,
From which most grateful wonder we should
    draw;
While chestnuts from the mountains of Thibet
Convey a lesson we should ne'er forget,
Of Wisdom Personal and most august,
In which through life we all should place our
    trust.
For there in buds minute are still contain'd
Incipient flowers and leaves, with health main-
    tain'd,
In microscopic smallness, whole, entire,
As those which later we must all admire.
Nor this alone, of God's surprising care,
Exists,—an instance never wanting, rare;
For, when transplanted to our climates cold,
A foreign cloak each wears, as you behold—
A garment warm, and suited to the air,
Which in its native woods it will not bear.
What evidence of Personal, free will
So potent, skilful, and benignant still!
What were it if you tried, in single leaves,
To mark the wonders nature ever weaves;
The aggregations of their diverse parts,
The nerve which union to the whole im-
    parts;

Enabling leaflets to be interlaced
Of which the hairy roots below are traced;
The wood so form'd with fibrile incrustation,
The bark so split to aid the germination,
The buds, prepared, to be expanded grown,
Push'd by an Agent whom we call "Unknown?"

And then what care in blending colours bright,
Which follows rules that artists know are right;
Each ground selected so as to display
The traced design in most effective way,
The flowers destined to be seen most near
Like painted miniatures by man appear,
While flowering shrubs to please the eye from far
Are roughly sketch'd with hues that never jar.
Each tint distributed with deepest skill
The ends of art most strictly to fulfil.
Nay, stranger yet, all this was wrought for man,
With whose formation flowers first began.
Before his birth the earth had seen no fruit,
No tree, no shrub, no floret that could suit
His sense of beauty, or his thirst assuage,
As is attested on Creation's page.
In that first period vegetable mould
Produced no fair forms gracious to behold.
While mushrooms high as mountains raise their
        heads;
Moss over all, one dull vast forest spreads;
One wild, prodigious, uniform mass
Of vegetation, with gigantic grass,

Prepared for future ages all that vein
Of coal which should man's industry sustain,
And also served to purify the air
For him and creatures to be later there.
So basking now in Heaven's blue smile, we see
How all was done with great benignity.

Let me then sing, amidst these changing leaves,
Of that High Wisdom which man here perceives,
As animating, ruling nature round,
And which in all its products still is found,
The supernatural, Eternal Mind,
Who counts each leaf that's ruffled by the wind,
Which rules omnipotent; to every eye
Display'd in things intelligible, high,
Passing beyond all floating objects here
To heights supernal, there to disappear.

Let never-ending hymns of joy ascend,
Majestic praises of what has no end.
Astonishment as happy as profound
In blissful hearts and minds should now be found.
Auroral splendour leading us to home
Proclaims unseen a vast supernal dome,
Where in gradation infinite will move
All nature, subject to Eternal Love,
From inorganic matter to the spheres
Where angel life the Deity reveres.
Oh, for the wing of Calderon! to bear
Our souls transported through this brilliant air,

That what can not be seen, or heard, or thought,
May to our heart and bosoms all be brought.

An English poet, famed in recent times
For lofty wisdom taught in simple rhymes,
Maintain'd that verse, more apt than other speech,
The ends of high philosophy could reach.
And sooth, the ancients loved in solemn song
To soar through regions which to truth belong ;
Though we, who live in more prosaic days,
Deem floral sweetness the sole test of lays.
Menander, Pindar, Ovid, too, as well,
Lucretius—truths of science all would tell,
Which proves at least that they deem'd apt and
    free
To poets fields of all philosophy.
'Tis true (though this diverts me from my way)
We now heed little what the ancients say.
"The thought escapes me," says a critic bold [4],
"That in this combat 'twixt the spirit old
And that which now as new the world pursues,
Sooner or later must the ancient lose,
If not the battle, still at least a wing
Of its great army, as a routed thing.
It is a fear sinistrous I express ;
For such an issue I no wish profess,
Yea, Heaven's my witness, but I needs must feel
That this is what the future will reveal.

[4] Saint Beuve.

The human mind seems hurried more and more
By a new current from the ancient shore—
For ever henceforth driven in a course,
And thence to return left without resource,
Which separates it from all classic thought
That Greece and Rome in former ages taught—
A change affecting literature all,
But chiefly what Philosophy we call.
I feel assured," he adds, " there will be left
But small minorities, not quite bereft
Of their traditions, which I would preserve,
And never wish that we from them should swerve.
Such is my vow ; but also such my fear,
That this result for Europe now is near."

The Supernatural for Greece and Rome
Existed as a true and common home,
From which they soar'd o'er grave, majestic Prose,
To which they flew back, seeking sweet repose
In dramas, fables, lofty epic songs,
Convinced that to the Muse such ground belongs.
But let me cite an instance—only one—
And to our course immediate I am gone.
Now Aristotle least of all was found
To haunt the precincts of mysterious ground ;
Yet thinks he not to err when he relates
What Cicero in after ages states ;
How his own friend, Eudemus, on his way
To Macedonia, was constrain'd to stay

At Pheras, falling sick, in Thessaly,
Then all oppress'd by cruel tyranny,
An Alexander, raging with fell might
To work all wrong, and outrage law and right.
Abandon'd by physicians, in a dream
A handsome youth to enter there did seem,
Who that he shortly would recover said,
That very soon the tyrant would be dead;
And then, that after he should five years roam,
He would return to his own native home.
"And so it all fell out," then adds the sage,
(That Aristotle, who has left the page,)
Restored Eudemus found himself to health;
His very brother murder'd by mere stealth
That tyrant; and when five years were all past
Eudemus hoped to see his home at last,
To Cyprus sailing back from Sicily,
According to the vision he did see;
When fighting in a battle he was slain;
But deem not, therefore, that his hopes were
    vain.
For Cicero, who quotes, takes care to add
The deep instruction that is thereby had;
For hence, he says, we learn now that the soul
Of thát Eudemus, when escaping sole,
And leaving flesh in which it had sojourn'd,
Then to his home had really return'd—
To that sweet native home which each would
    see,
And, as old sages deem'd, eternally.

This can suffice to hint what lay below
The surface from which ancient thoughts would
    grow.
You see the gulf of which the critic speaks,
The contrast which humanity now seeks ;
The ground laid open, which explains his fear
Lest classic thoughts for us may disappear.

But how I wander, as with time to spare,
Describing circles in the boundless air,
As if not sped to seek a distant goal
With strength reserved and never-bending soul.
Straight onwards henceforth all our flight should be
To the far fields of real mystery.
Still ere thus borne off by determined will
A last small circle we may flap in still ;
For when some would divert us from our way
By flinging missiles, this we needs must say—
That all the paths which genius ever trod
Have never bent to men from showing God.
Dante, and Dryden, Pope himself, did sing
On moral themes ; to truth did homage bring.
And elements you thought would ne'er combine
They melt together, causing them to shine
In one vast glory of eternal light
Beyond the reach of all our human sight.
Ethereal subjects they would not reject,
As if theology did not reflect
The one thing needed by the poet's song—
That type for which he too on earth must long—

Of beauty absolute, the poesy
Of that which still invisible must be.
The Muse sings not to sections, but to all
The human race on which her eyes must fall;
To man, and not a part, but to the whole,
His reason, fancy, mind, and heart, and soul;
To childhood, youth, maturity and age;
Her song must hear the simple and the sage.
So what affects them all, in each degree,
Will with the ends of poetry agree.
And since the supernatural is found
Surrounding all, it is the Muse's ground,
Perfumed with flowers, scene for highest art,
And bright with dews to fructify the heart,
O'er which far echoes then will soar and wait,
As if come down from ante-natal state.
Though still least sings she for the servile crew
Who pagan fancies only would renew.
No wave that breaks upon the rugged shore,
Which does not cast upon it richer store
Of inspirations fitter for the Muse
Than the mere fables which the ancients use
Of Neptune and his old eternal train,
To yield stale images to poets vain.
Let the traditions of the ancient world
Still shine upon our banners all unfurl'd;
But let not that which did defeat their aim
E'er taint our flag with its dishonour'd name.
The Christian Supernatural can yield
A brighter meadow than Parnassian field.

For three immortal Muses hover there ;
True Freedom, Faith, and Love, will fan the air.
All feeling generous, all lofty thought,
With them, and them alone, must now be sought.
If you deny this, speed you to Japan,
And there behold what is abandon'd man,
Possessing taste and genius with his tribe,
But in his faith a thing we can't describe.

Then hear me sing what is stupendous, high,
Affecting all and each with interest nigh ;
Though seldom subject to the human sight,
In thought's last limits lies its puissant might.
The unseen world reveal'd should prove a theme
Like gorgeous wonders in a youthful dream ;
Though still not swerving from severest line,
We seek but truth exactly to divine [s].

There is inherent in our nature deep
A love which art can seldom cast to sleep,
Impelling us to seek what lies beyond
All earthly objects of affection fond.
The supernatural is what we call
This end mysterious, which is sought by all.
In vain from this the sceptic seeks to fly ;
Discarding reason, still it follows nigh,

[s] The line of argument is in great part borrowed from the
work of Mozley on Miracles.

In wildest forms and contravening sense
To prove his vaunted boasts are all pretence.
The man of wit becomes, with judgment cool,
As if of mountebanks he were the tool ;
While others, humble and to nature true,
Accept her wholly, let what may ensue.
This great emotion, follow'd to its spring,
Reveals a light which oft makes poets sing,
Uprising from that sense within each mind
Eternal life to realize and find ;
The least faint token of the world unseen
Seems to disclose whate'er may intervene,
Existence personal abiding there,
To follow which from earth would each one dare.
Rightly or wrongly at such signs we grasp,
As if our safety rested on that clasp,
To fear no more absorption of the grave,
From which it yields a guarantee to save.
Excess, though morbid in this longing, still
Can prove that this is no fictitious will.
It speaks of Being in another life
Beyond this present of continued strife ;
Of Being personal on unseen throne,
Who can and will with Him prolong our own.

'Tis true such love when merely curious, fond,
Leads to no real good this earth beyond.
" If they resist the Prophets," it is said,
" They will not hear one risen from the dead."

But in itself it is a useful spring
To meet obstructions and our souls to wing.
It wakens, solemnizes human thought,
Inspires action even though unsought.
We see the endless world then with our eyes,
And blind affection for the finite dies.
A miracle produces wonder more
Than all the marvels of mere Nature's store.
Though you great Nature's forces all combine,
They cast no shadow where this light will shine;
For this directly pierces to the soul,
And to the sense which comprehends the whole;
Including man's immortal future end,
To which it then his motives all will bend;
While Nature's marvels only show a part
Which cannot this way ever touch his heart;
For wonders physical can only show
What things around us real are below;
They do not tell us we are not, as they,
The passing pageant of an ending day.
Of love like this, then, let us soar to sing,
And plume for flight a bold, confiding wing.

The earth had seen successions many, vast,
Of life in plants and animals all past,
When a new Being made his entrance strange
In nature, suited to a higher range;
Since he alone on earth is that which knows,
And knowledge such, a thing unearthly shows.

With this appearance of created man,
For him the reign of miracles began.
His sense of God, his consciousness, free will,
In an unknowing world all matter still,
Alone in Nature cast abruptly so—
Surpass'd all previous wonders here below.
Accordant, therefore, with his wondrous birth,
Reserved for him were visions not of earth,
The Supernatural almost to see,
Where Nature's borders end in mystery.
That, too, which at her portals ever stands,
Which he alone detects and understands,
As showing near the Universal Mind,
In all the traces he is sure to find
Of some design to which great Nature yields,
Track'd to the edge of true mysterious fields,
Himself inserted, as is proved by prayer,
Within a world, though with his end not there,
In close relation to another life,
With present things constrain'd to be at strife;
By situation an anomaly,
Things beyond Nature he is call'd to see.
A sense religious is to all men given,
To believe it just logicians must be driven;
For when some sophist will this fact deny,
Enough for them to hear great Nature's cry.
Religion then alone can fully prove
That when man dies he can but hence remove
To worlds unseen from which that sense descends,
To fit him here for some great future ends.

He moves on earth ; his home is in the skies ;
Of both he wears a mark that never dies.
So thus existing in divided state,
He well may foster expectations great
Of finding here below more wonders high
Than lower creatures use or can descry ;
And so, religion, nature, he will find
Abound in tokens of Omniscient Mind,
That by high miracles demand assent
When what surpasses Nature here is sent.

But now, descending from these regions high,
Let us observe the men who this deny,
The Supernatural rejecting all,
Whom courteously philosophers we call ;
Though their objections, sweet Heaven knows, ap-
    pear
As no great proof of wisdom when seen near ;
No sign, at least, that they are used to love
The facts which train our thoughts to fly above
The world that's seen, in which with all their
    pains
Is found no food that highest life sustains ;
Unless to be content to think and die,
Is deem'd the end of true philosophy—
Unless " the womb of inessential thought "
Be the last bourne Philosophy has sought.

Let's see who then approach to overthrow
Whate'er as supernatural we know.

They answer, " Friends ;" But friends of whom?
    we ask ;
Intent on warfare, they may wear a mask.
'Tis well to give us sign and countersign,
As in Spain's " *Philothea the Divine.*"
'Tis well to know of each distinct the name,
Lest friend and enemy be deem'd the same.
The first who answers, as with Calderon,
Is Antitheos, and from India flown.
When, like a blow on Faith's sweet, comely face,
Words fall fiercely all belief to efface
In one great Power, Primal Source of Love,
And in the soul's immortal life above.
Next comes up the World, thoughtless, full of
    scorn
For all those truths he deems are lowly born ;
So things first known to shepherds and the poor
Are, above all, what he can not endure.
The Supernatural besides must be
What with his habits never can agree ;
He deems our theme but vulgar at the best,
And with closed eyes proceeds to take his rest.
Voluptuousness then will turn aside,
In order her dissenting smiles to hide ;
As the true wise, supreme she tries to pass,
Too oft successful we must own, alas !
Although, if rightly understood and felt,
Her hostile weapons would to friendly melt.
But to the understanding she hints need
Of being by inquiring spirits freed

From all that would confine or else coerce
Those who from wrong would stray to the re-
    verse.
Then who come next, protesting all is right,
Bearing on banners, *"After darkness light?"*
These with the others blended form the host,
Who now, though torn, are here brought forward
    most ;
While each more fix'd, determined than the rest,
Is a foe subtle, as the clubs attest.
In fact, the best disguised, most artful foe,
Is he who boasts he can exactly know
All things divine, and by *inquiry free,*
The root and crown of his divinity.
But while disguised he passes with a sign,
A creed presenting much like yours and mine,
The Supernatural affords a test
Which proves at length the surest and the best ;
For when his antecedents you demand,
The countersign you quickly understand
Is wanting, when the Sacramental sense
Is found to give implacable offence.
With questions from the first, this foe was arm'd,
Still seeking those who might by them be harm'd ;
He neither believed nor disbelieved aught,
While ill at ease within, he boldly fought.
With doubts and scoffs the Faith he still defied,
And all acknowledged mysteries denied.
Men call'd him Spirit of Inquiry free,
Or Understanding, that must all things see ;

But now, while passing under other name,
His triumph Reason finds a thing of shame.
These four combined, disguises when cast off,
Will spurn our theme and at our reasons scoff;
But nathless let us meet now all array'd
These sons of battle, calm and undismay'd,
Who wishing war, or pleasure, or their pay,
Will come prepared, their forces to assay.

Now first they think that Nature's order all
Excludes what mortals superhuman call.
Her facts repeated show at work a cause
Which makes them think that permanent are laws.
But what demonstrates permanency so?
Nothing that we or they themselves can know.
They think the future must be like the past,
But here for logic they proceed too fast.
In point of fact the future is a blank,
Though what is gone assumes the foremost rank.
Still as we walk, the past alone in sight,
What lies before us is as dark as night.
That this should be is but an impulse given
Without intelligence—direct from Heaven;
For, left without it, acts of men would stop,
And doubt's dark curtain o'er all living drop.
The trust is needed; but no reason can
Demonstrate it as sure to thinking man;
In reason, therefore, having no foundation,
The ground is gone for further disputation

D

To show that Nature's order thus can yield
For scouting miracles a proper field.
Since Nature's order lasting can't be proved,
Of its cessations doubts must be removed.
By reason's process you cannot instil
That what has happen'd, happen ever will.
So miracles, supposing it to cease,
From heeding them can grant you no release.
Unlikeness to experience proves no law
From which with reason you objections draw ;
Philosophy proclaims its own defect,
And shows that Reason likeness can't expect.
If reason be their ground, unlikeness then
Should not by reason puzzle thoughtful men.
Your fact may be anomalous and new,
But Reason says it yet may all be true.
Induction would affect to play the part
Of a resistless universal art,
From one fact proved to generalize ever,
But Reason will approve such usage never.
Induction scientific here must end ;
You're ruled by Instinct when you words expend ;
And Reason bids you to resist it when
You hear attested miracles by men.
'Tis Reason should prevail and make you see
That Instinct yields to what is mystery.
Experience is a principle of use ;
But here alone 'tis open to abuse.
To this belongs not speculative space,
Urging what can and what can not take place,

Controlling Faith religious, to deny
What God for man determines from on high.
Induction thus transmuted issues out
Not truth, but fiction, maugré all its doubt,
An airy weapon in a giant's hand,
Which as a shadow each one can withstand;
The unsubstantial thrust conveys no shock,
At such a warlike implement we mock.

The Supernatural, resisted long,
Has been opposed by able men and strong;
The battle rages still with all its might,
While heroes oft will join the mystic fight.
Great men they are, acute and learned still,
But yet by Reason they can't have their will.
It is a weapon only that they want,
A Universal, after all their vaunt.
Unbelief's logic has not yet that found;
So all its strength is wielded for a sound,
But wasted still on a fictitious blade
That proves in war no better than a shade.

But what has caused such logical defect?
Alas! it is not what we could expect.
The Muse herself, the sweetest friend of man,
Must own her guilt and leave it if she can.
Imagination seizes feelings strong,
And then diverts them to a purpose wrong.

D 2

Induction she exaggerates until
'Tis used an object worthless to fulfil ;
Unreasoning instinct seems to reason changed,
With universal propositions ranged
To prove that Nature's order, changeless ever,
Departure from it can admit of never.

And is it thus, O kind and noble friend,
That thou thy priceless energies wilt spend ?
Imagination, what can tempt thee so,
To whom such greatness and such bliss we owe ?
By thy internal force we see the truth
Of glorious visions that ennoble youth.
By thee we grasp at things external just ;
In selfish feeling we disdain to trust ;
By thee we understand the wants of others,
And burst the web that admiration smothers.
By thee we sympathize with all that's good,
Which reason lonely never understood.
Yea, more, thou art in truth a diver bold,
Whom nothing from the depths can ever hold,
Met by pure Science straying at their brink,
Met in the gulfs profound by those who sink ;
In conic sections and in calculation
Of probabilities, and in gradation ;
In differential, integral as well,
Infinitesimal, as sages tell ;
In logarithms algebra applied
To geometry, thou still can be descried ;

So Mathematics, when thus touch'd by thee,
Become in greatest minds true Poesy.
Without thy aid all Science is like lead
Lodged in a deep but deaf and eyeless head.
'Tis thou that teachest to combine, invent,
Construct, accomplishing our high intent.
Not Reason, but a far diviner part,
'Tis thou that art the mistress of our heart.
And wilt thou then consent this way to yield
Submissive, vanquish'd fly thy native field?
Grasp'd thus and master'd by ideas cold,
Resign'd to try the part of Reason bold?
Thou art not then thyself a noble power,
But a poor puppet fretting for an hour,
Our nature's weakness, simply its disgrace,
For all thy smiling, harmless, placid face.
When active, thou canst human weakness scorn;
When passive, better thou hadst ne'er been born.
When used aright 'tis godlike that thou art,
While God in Reason cannot have a part.
In God, I think, there can no Reason be;
'Tis not by syllogism that He will see;
So Intuition is our highest gift,
While Reason will with reasons all things sift.
Reason is but the crutch of our weak mind,
Which in it can assistance needful find;
But thou, Imagination, needst no stay
While onwards fearless thou canst pierce thy way.
And wilt thou yield submissive to thy foe?
From that time forward thou canst nothing know;

For then thou art delusion and a snare,
To make grave men the vilest things to dare.
Materialism even is thy child,
Dress'd in cold Reason's garb by fancy wild.
'Tis thou that thinkest atoms to detect
In action, as Lucretius did expect—
Spontaneous, voluntary, making all
To spring to life obedient to their call ;
As if the bodies void of life when whole
By being pulverized obtain'd a soul ;
Such particles and fragments turn'd to dust
Become a vital principle to trust,
A changed diameter sufficing so
To make mere matter like a spirit know !
Impress'd by matter thou art helpless then
To see the spiritual ruling men ;
And thus impossible thou deemest all
The wonders high that miracles we call.

Then Custom too, another friend of man,
Is oft enlisted in the slavish clan
Who cannot break the trammels cast around
By habits which they deem all reasons sound.
Custom, that sweet and humble constant guide,
Makes all things safe and pleasant at our side.
And this is her great service to our race—
Abrupt eccentric actions to efface.
To render easy, happy, constant, sound,
The steps we take upon the roughest ground.

But when with leaden mace she deadens sense
Of wonder, and deems novelty pretence,
Making the loftiest hearts both hard and blind
The Supernatural to mark and find,
Then is she Reason's foe, a conscript fit
To swell the legions which deem scoffing wit;
The Demon's most familiar liege-man known
Being the world which has around them grown.
Lo! the dull vulgar, who sweet nature see
Graced with all beauty and sublimity.
Her glories, stale, they pass them heedless by,
Or gaze with vacant unadmiring eye.
But what is worse, we will not see a fact
If our own custom it would counteract.
Then wonders are explain'd away with scorn,
As not by us beheld since we were born;
So that miracles should be disbelieved,
Should less surprise than if they were re-
    ceived.
For Reason isolated, midst a host
Of influences causing vulgar boast—
Weight of custom, association's power,
With strength of passion which will sway the
    hour,
The vis inertiæ of torpid mind,
The spectacle of Nature ever kind
In Uniformity's majestic file—
Which thus interpreted can men beguile,
All serving to make up that blind world's will
Which Truth's great objects never can fulfil,

Finds herself then benumb'd and quite suppress'd,
However proudly she may then be dress'd.

Well here the Muses, oft by Reason scorn'd,
Descend to aid her, by their counsels warn'd.
Reason needeth Faith, itself to believe,
When mere impressions seek it to deceive;
While Faith is Reason with its limits known,
Which, when 'tis sound, it never will disown.
Our Reason becomes Faith, in common life,
Unless with mankind we would be at strife;
In Science even it would often yield
To those who merely strong denials wield;
It needs a principle of Faith to trust
Its own conclusion, howsoever just.
But now observe how Reason, once set free,
The Supernatural will clearly see.

Creation first the ancients all denied;
And now what has become of that old pride?
Hume, in a foot-note, sends it away thus,
Whole ages' nightmare, with no greater fuss,
By simply saying that this maxim old—
" Nihil fit ex nihilo," although bold,
Now ceases to be held within the school
Where Reason and Philosophy can rule.
Matter's creation then may be allow'd,
Whate'er denials had before been vow'd.
The God that's personal is seen once more,
The God of Faith, as in Patristic lore.

For miracles, solutions two are given;
To one or other we are ever driven.
The one an easy, gradual descent—
To trace to legends all the whole event;
The other steep, abrupt, resisted still—
To see in them a Personal free will.
The first we choose, suspecting Reason's voice,
As if such fear could justify our choice;
Confounding truths beyond our Reason's ken
With airy visions not design'd for men;
We choose the second when we rise in mind,
And let our Reason mere impressions bind,
Knowing her veto has not been pronounced,
Though Feelings merely have to be renounced.
So, thus deliver'd, Reason now is free,
More than in Pagan times, these truths to see.
Unlike ideas in those ancient schools,
'Tis Reason pure that simply grandly rules.
Conceptions of philosophers recede,
While of more childlike notions men feel need.
The Primitive, Poetical, returns;
With Reason's light the Fancy even burns.
With Brahman notions men will not compare
The God who numbers and who weighs each hair,
Who every five or six years can renew
Without submitting aught to tenant's view,
The house they live in, from roof to the base,
While they His silent action never trace,
And doubt if He can ever elsewhere raise,
Howe'er unknown and wondrous be His ways,

That Edifice when fallen to the ground
Which to men's eyes on earth no more is found.
Him this Pure Reason bids us all adore,
On childlike wings to Heaven upwards soar.
Reason has shown her strength ; but then observe,
From Christian limits she no more will swerve.
Back on herself that strength she now will turn ;
As her own critic will her pure light burn,
So proving for her force the safest check,
When all the rest is darkness and a wreck.

But mark still further how this cause is strong,
And all the wonders which to it belong.
Can laws material, physical, give way
To any Being Spiritual ? say.
Be this conceivable or not, reply,
The fact is shown each day to ev'ry eye.
The laws of matter are suspended thus
By laws of life, as all may see in us.
Our spirits move our bodies to fulfil
The slightest impulse of our simple will.
To mount up to heaven or to step on ground,
Is inconceivable by Reason found.
Alike incredible, the one can be
Proved true by walking, as a child can see.
Then how should Incredulity rely
Upon itself when tempted to deny
The other instance, as in Scripture found,
And not feel tremble all its boasted ground ?

But more than this ; for Nature's order here
Should make us think that wonders will appear—
Divine suspensions of material law—
From which alone this inference we draw.
For all these laws we know that now prevail
Are still arranged in an ascending scale.
Thus matter inorganic first is seen ;
Then laws of vegetation intervene ;
Then, by a leap enormous, laws of life
That's animal, with hope, and fear, and strife ;
Above these still the laws of moral being
For creatures that have higher gifts than feeling.
Suppose a Being with intelligence,
Who has experience only in the sense
Of lower classes in this scale of laws,
Beyond whose bounds he never knowledge draws,
Then such would be unable to conceive
The acts which higher classes all perceive.
A thinking stone could never then be found
Explaining why it left its local ground ;
While still man's hand would all its mind defy
When sending it to wander in the sky.
No granite thinking ever could explain
Explosions caused within its hardest vein,
By law of chemistry producing shocks
Which all its knowledge then defies and mocks.
A thinking mineral confined to sloth
Would not believe the vegetable growth.
A thinking vegetable with surprise
Would see life animal and proof despise.

A thinking animal would still refuse
To take in truths which it could never use.
Thus backward laws progressive in succession
Can be conceived in limitless digression,
But forward view'd, 'tis mystery profound,
A dark, and pathless, and forbidden ground.
Therefore ascending, when we come to man,
Disprove a higher action if you can,
As much above him in the wondrous scale
As to approach him lower creatures fail.
No. For once Shakspeare nods when Hamlet
    cries
That man, as highest, nature all defies,
Because, forsooth, at present nothing higher
He can behold to cause him to admire !
But is it certain that an Ant or Bee
Our presence moving can detect and see ?
With smoke or water we can change their
    state,
While they attribute all their woes to Fate.
Then we can be affected too just so
By higher beings whom we do not know.
We pass 'midst creatures to our beauty blind ;
There may soar near us what we never find.
And since the seen world microscopic shows
Marvels at which our wonder ever grows,
To find things greater still we are prepared
Beyond what to conceive our fancy dared,
In that life higher, wholly hidden here,
Where Perfect Love and Beauty will appear,

Towards which by gravitation's central law
Eternal Love will spheres celestial draw.
Analogy will teach that this must be,
And thus throw light on fields of mystery.

So we arrive again by other roads
At God and Spirits in unseen abodes.
That Will supreme and personal as well
Must henceforth doubts of miracles dispel.
Not empty then of Nature's King the throne,
The great Free Agent Reason thus will own,
Under Him his wonders to disbelieve
Is with vain words our own minds to deceive.

But miracles have ceased, we oft are told
By some who love to use assertions bold.
Here a distinction Reason will propose,
Whatever modern sages may suppose.
That miracles had ceased, the Fathers say,
While still they cry they see them in their day,
Proclaiming them as wonders from on high,
Attesting truths, and helping to descry
What Scripture miracles had plainer proved,
Though sooth from their own present times re-
    moved.
Now this is still what Reason understands
When deep attention any one commands.
The wisest men will not from this line swerve
While saying they have ceased, with a reserve ;

And this implies they believe they can be
Yet proved by cautious human testimony.
That they are possible they still maintain ;
And absolute denials they count vain.
Their grave reserve is thus a weighty thing,
Enabling them to evidence to bring
A mind prepared for truth on any day,
Coming then strangely as it ever may.
In this reserve of Reason we descry
What only fools are tempted to deny—
The skirts of arguments, portentous, just
Borders of regions in which mind will trust.
But if, still following the Fathers' way,
Seeming at times the contrary to say,
The first great miracles they will not dare
With hodiernal wonders to compare—
It is that, like them, they conceive fulfill'd
The end for which the former ones were will'd.
Those were but tools in the Almighty's plan,
To teach at first the Gospel unto man.
Take any tool and look at it alone—
It seems unmeaning as a thing unknown ;
But as a key it serves still to unlock
What would without it all your efforts mock.
These miracles were instruments to show
What Reason otherwise could never know—
That doctrines wise and suited to the heart
Were not of individuals a part ;
Good, but perhaps enthusiasm pure,
Which could not be expected to endure—

But that from God in heaven they were taught,
Who to instruct and save His creatures sought.
These miracles were needed at the first,
That light supernal might on mankind burst.
And so far they regard them as the past,
Without ascribing limits to the Vast.
We live at present amidst powers great,
Which constitute for all the Christian state,
Resulting from that agency employ'd
Of which the end will never be destroy'd.
That end achieved, such means we want no more,
At least as much as men in days of yore ;
The Building raised, the key-stone in its place,
Supports and scaffolding will leave no trace ;
In this way, the distinction is avow'd
By all who are to Reason liege-men vow'd.
But when substantial evidence is brought,
And that still wonders happen we are taught,
Reason says it must be believed as well,
And so, convinced, admits of what you tell.
Our argument will suffer no restraint ;
It is our belief that will feel constraint.
Sage Pascal, Mozley, both maintain and hold
The new are credible as were the old.
To think that this dishonours what was done
You have authority or Reason none.
In truth, a purpose always is fulfill'd,
When hodiernal miracles are will'd ;
They still proclaim the Being Personal
Who moves behind accomplishing them all.

The world unseen is still what they disclose,
Impressions causing more than some suppose;
The fact external gives no rest to mind;
It passes onwards awed, its God to find;
It is no longer "*one world at a time*,"
As when we hear of fools the noisy chime,
It *is*, sooth, two worlds welded into one;
But this is fact when all is said and done;
For view the seen world ever as you will,
The two are join'd in mystic borders still.
The world that moves is not, as Poets say,
Repelling rays from the supernal Day,
"The only nurse of all things that we know,"
As if, like plants, upon the earth we grow.
'Tis not "the mother of all things we feel,"
As if our brain and heart were but as steel;
We know and feel, far far beyond that store,
And scent the fragrance of the unseen shore,
Uniting firmest Faith in what shall be
With love intense for that which now we see.

But then with doctrines this whole sphere of
        thought,
So closely blended, always must be sought;
And this is what gives pain to many now,
As with loud tongues they plainly will avow.
They say 'tis Doctrines make men persecute—
A maxim which their argument may suit;
Though of a truth it vanishes in air
If to hear both sides they can only bear;

For Christian doctrines would extirpate roots
Of all the evils that can yield such fruits;
While mere philanthropists do but complain,
Monotonously urging what is vain,
Saying, "We want no doctrines, love is all,"
And this is what philosophy they call!

Let's hear what Reason calm has then to say.
Before we follow on this vulgar way.

How vain are words when facts like Heaven's own
    fire
Still light up beacons mankind to inspire!
Take the most civilized and perfect state—
It shows no sign on this point to debate
With sophists who all doctrines would deny,
While reasoning sages pass them calmly by;
The bulk of men will doctrines not reject,
Whatever some still vainly may expect.
While Poets find congenial with the Muse
The very phrases which Scholastics use,
Faith's holy doctrines can so intertwine
With hearts and feelings such as yours and mine—
Some proof that they belong unto the whole
Of what should animate the human soul,
When once it would expand its noble wings,
And gaze with rapture on supernal things,
With one glimpse ravish'd, contemplating all,
While joy transcendent will adoring fall.

E

'Tis not a gloomy shadow, void of life,
Which now descends amidst our mingled strife,
To blight the blossoms of our early spring,
Or on the rest a noxious vapour fling ;
It rather is a sweet and gentle trace
Of Nature's primal and Elysian face.
It is not irksome webs around us spun—
It is a light diviner than the sun
E'er pours with splendour on the common earth—
The earnest of a new and glorious birth,
Gilding the waves of time and all we see—
Pure Faith and Nature join'd with ecstacy,
High Truth and Beauty in one radiant shrine—
All that we love with all that is divine ;
As if bright Iris o'er the dusky grass
Had cast her colour'd rays on all who pass.
If you suppose we hail another tone,
The light is ours, the darkness is your own.
Above and not below this Nature seen,
Heard, felt, and loved, is therefore what we mean,
Its sounds all music and its visions bright,
Its thoughts are glory and its actions light ;
All wondrous, superhuman, gracious, high,
Unmoved they stand while all the rest must die.

Then think not doctrines cast a shadow here ;
They teach but love, which to all hearts is dear.
Without that love they are unmeaning things,
While with it they are plumes of azure wings,

Which soar aloft, though you distinguish not
The lines precise which constitute each spot.
Yet deem not their distinctions void of sense,
As if with them Religion could dispense;
Of human progress doctrine is the base,
Without which soon is lost the boasted race.
It is for action higher level gain'd
A motive, strength, with nought unduly strain'd.
To give up doctrine is to retrograde,
To give up vantage-ground that has been
    made,
To leave a later for an early stage
Of that humanity we would assuage
By proudly taking from it food and rest
Wherewith alone it can be fed and blest;
It is exchanging power o'er the heart
For what had never touch'd its inmost part,
A motive spring of action, constant, sure,
For what in no past ages did endure.
So, when men speculate, they wish to leave
All doctrines as mere things that will deceive;
But when 'tis practical results they want,
Recalling them, they drop their empty vaunt,
All founded on a thought mistaken, vain,
Respecting doctrines and what they contain.
For nothing perfect or complete is known
When we have caught their deep and constant
    tone.
If men reduce a knowledge to an art,
Then uniform and round they make each part;

But where the Supernatural must dwell
Abrupt is much ; and we know nothing well.
O altitudo ! in Divinity
Expresses all the knowledge that can be.
When men a total seek, while still confined
To but a part, they must possess a mind
Contented with presumption, and supplies
From supposition's groundless, senseless cries ;
But doctrines which the Church would have us
    know,
Are never multiplied and rounded so.
Few and majestic, high, beyond our reach,
Like Alpine summits, all they ever teach
Is admiration, pleasure, and amaze,
As towards their cloud-capp'd peaks we upwards
    gaze ;
And as for persecutions, which some say
Must always follow where our doctrines sway,
Their argument a dull oblivion needs,
Since those raged most who sought to cancel
    creeds.
In hearts, not doctrines, lay the mischief sad.
When forced, than good men, we like better
    bad—
Yes, better outcasts, harlots, or profane,
Than pure ascetics who use God in vain.
But now some seek to deify our race,
And thereby ancient doctrines all efface.
But this is height and never depth as well ;
So, wanting truth, it sooth has nought to tell.

Opposed to facts of Nature, it must end
In vapid aspirations, which all tend
To weaken true solidity in man
By vainest issues and without a plan.
The doctrines proved by miracles at first
Are those alone in which he still can trust.
'Tis they which quite changed the world that we
    see,
And made our life a tender mystery—
A stage so unlike that Pagan world old,
Of which the shame has never yet been told;
For what produced this change but doctrines
    plain,
Which superseded all past teaching vain?
Humiliation of th' Eternal Word,
Which to the angels falling seem'd absurd;
Which made them then reject their destined
    Queen,
Like later sophists as submission mean—
Despised humanity of God to believe—
Such doctrines Pride at no time would receive.
Yet what did they produce? You know it all
If only Pagan evidence you call.
Just take an instance, from Lactantius drawn,
That witness to the Truth at early dawn.
" See," he exclaims, " how humble, equitable,
Are now these Christians in their faith so stable;
See what equality amongst them there
In rich and poor, and then, oh! then, com-
    pare."

But all this moral structure has for base
The doctrines once imparted to our race.
It is but from them—yes, from them alone—
That all our manners, all our rights have grown.
From God Incarnate, and Atonement made,
The rest will follow as from bodies shade.
The Supernatural lights all our creed ;
But man of this old element has need.
This gets all ground, and keeps it too as well ;
And so its end is never hard to tell.
For that which gains, ne'er loses in time's roll,
Must, we should think, at last obtain the whole.

But now to close the sage's mighty book *,
Abroad, around us, let us only look,
To see the Supernatural in life
Amidst the long protracted mortal strife,
As witness'd less in scientific guise
Than in what strikes with rapture Poets' eyes.
Sooth, if the Supernatural is found
To constitute indeed the Poet's ground,
We might perhaps have bade all Science pass,
To yield to what its powers will surpass.
Science climbs up its ladder by degrees,
Poesy mounts on wings and pure Truth sees.
With one extension of its glorious wing
It gains the heights, and can, immortal, sing.

* Mozley.

Science examines, tries, and searches long ;
What yesterday was right, to-day is wrong ;
Athenian Chrysippus "*who all things knew,*"
Did he now live, must all begin anew.
Each man of science, in one long succession,
Has felt the need in his path of suppression ;
His predecessors one by one have stray'd
From truth in points where great mistakes were
      made.
All in their turns immensely are surpass'd,
While what the Muses crown will ever last.
Laplace, Lavoisier, have now to yield
Their place to later comers to their field.
Erasure is the work of Science still ;
For self-correction is its endless will.
But Homer, Pindar, Shakspeare, victors calm,
No time can bend their tall aërial palm.
Yea, Virgil's Dido sits upon a throne
As fix'd as Nature, with man's heart her own.

If this great Law applied be used as test,
The Supernatural will prove what's best—
What nought can weaken, no discovery stains,
What question'd triumphs, what resisted, reigns,
Through all the generations of our race,
Of God and truth one vast eternal trace.
Would you now seek examples ? they abound ;
Lo ! one, which in an instant can be found.
" Oh !" cries an ancient writer, famed of old
For thoughts profound, quite simply, quaintly told,

" Belief in God's a thing of beauty ever ;
A mortal tongue can sing its beauty never !
To meet with good men too 's a thing of joy
Beyond all language that we can employ "—
Words thus extorted by a sense of truth
From one who little heeded guiding youth.
Faith knows it all ; to Bards the whole she
    brings.
And grants them thus immeasurable wings.

The superhuman, sacramental mind,
Is all that Poets wish for, lofty, kind.
They too leave earth, and through the unseen
    soar ;
And what does this mind love and ask for more ?
For Poets teach, and ceaselessly instil
What this mysterious sense can grant and will,
The beauty of Creation, and the love
Which makes concordant earth and Heaven above,
From inorganic matter to the soul,
And upwards thence to Him who rules the
    whole—
Ascent surpassing sense and highest thought,
Protracted through all wonders He has wrought,
Comprising in its vast expansive sway
The youthful song, the praise that angels pay—
Profane so call'd and sacred, just the same,
Distinction counting but an empty name.
Eternal thoughts, with each day's lightest thing
Blended together, rise on purple wing,

Causing alliance which no discord taints
Between the people and their Poets, Saints—
For when before the altars they adore
They then can play as children did of yore,
Still, in presence of the Eternal Three,
Who reign in High Heaven, Blessed Trinity.
There's no confounding "*Latria*" in minds
Where each Creation's God in all things finds.
What does this sense of superhuman life
Impart to mankind 'midst their mortal strife?
All that poets, what even sages high
Would have them think—what only fools deny.
Yes; these great, lofty spirits will agree
With what was taught to us from infancy.
Profoundest sympathy those ever show
Who their own fearless strength the surest know.
Like you they pray; they palpitate, adore,
Love than all knowledge thinking to be more.
The want to love and believe dost thou feel?
To weep, to strike thy breast, to bow and kneel,
To stretch to Heaven serene confiding hands?
Hear only Genius—all it understands.
"Oh, goodness of the strong," a Poet cries,
"When to support our weakness thus it tries!"
Telling it to feel like us and believe,
What only vain, impatient spirits leave,
The doctrines of Redemption, pure, entire;
The Eucharist, which goodness will inspire;
The crime of those who venture to reject
A part or whole with some prevailing sect;

The will to spurn mere Pagan thoughts of God,
As if all things were ruled by Fortune's nod;
To teach them patience when afflictions frown;
To make them see in woe their future crown;
To cast a halo round all things in sight;
To grant them mystic armour for the fight;
The sacrificial offering of the Mass
A Jacob's ladder on which angels pass,
To fill them with true charity divine,
And make the earth with Heaven's own glory
    shine—
Their very formulas endued with grace
That's infantine, whose gentleness we trace
In all their words, and actions, and desires,
While God's own splendour secret thought at-
    tires,
His Justice only seeming to forget,
Upon His Mercy all their vision set,
Their thoughts like snow-white rivulets that dare
Entrust their waters to the golden air,
Like distant waves of an harmonious sound
Which roll with softness o'er a fragrant ground,
With Hope enthroned wherever they have pass'd;
What poets dreamt not, though so sweet, to last,
While living thenceforth free yet with control
Stronger than life to guard their anxious soul—
Such the result of super-earthly things—
Yes, such the strength and aid it ever brings.

But let us follow life as thus conceived
Through common scenes where Faith has been
  received.

In certain moods no praise is understood,
And least of all when given to the good.
At times the best man to admire strives ;
With others this vein lasts them all their lives.
Indifference like this itself is strange ;
With miracles you might its coolness range ;
It has results that palpably mislead,
Whatever be your notion or your creed.
To view the good and Catholicity,
And both unmoved and languidly to see,
Is just as great a wonder as to find
Men to celestial mechanism blind,
Deeming the sun and moon an empty show
Beyond them—all a farce the wish to know,
Revolving spheres and planets, fancies wild,
And each who heeds them but a frantic child.
Yet you, who feel your mind with genius burn,
Will have your days when this mood will return ;
As if against yourself there were reaction—
As if, within you, work'd a mean, base faction.
I will not call to aid celestial fire ;
To ask it here there's no one need aspire ;
Avaunt ! the low and grovelling spirits base,
Who cannot of themselves this folly trace.
I call alone at present on the soul
To feel the grandeur of the mighty whole.

It is a Poet only that we need,
It is to Song's sweet regions that we speed.
Descend, ye Muses, teach us now to soar,
To feel this sluggish torpor never more.

Then first the child is carried to the Font,
With life commencing his great mystic want;
While some, quite left to nature for their guide,
Deem no great harm the old infanticide.
A halo now of colour'd blissful light
Presents an angel to the altered sight.
Words solemn, holy, ancient, of the Priest,
Impress all now assisting at this feast
Of innocence, as if they were the fold
First made Disciples in the days of old.
The unseen world is then presented clear,
Almost as if its wonders did appear;
The rite accomplish'd, all exult to see
This child a Christian clad with mystery.
And oh! what vistas are thrown open then
Inviting those who wander thoughtless men!
They feel as if brought back to times of yore,
Resolving things they thought not of before—
Such power now issues from the holy strain,
Each hearer would commence his life again.
The Supernatural so potent, grand,
Has force no mortal wholly can withstand.
Resist it, yes, but still it sinks below;
More than is own'd, they think, they feel, they
    know.

Then later, and adapted to our years,
Clothed in soft beauty it again appears.
Oh! dry hard heart of age, thou needst must
    bow
To what will pass in clearest vision now.
Yes, heart of stone, from thee the tears will
    fall;
Once more, though late, thou comprehendest all.
Thou wilt not pass within the church's door;
But in the street Religion has her store
Of strange coincidences, to arrest
The eyes and steps of those who sigh for rest;
For thee, perhaps, with Providential care
Design'd, ordain'd, and granted to thee there.
For see these maidens fair, array'd in white,
A sweet, unearthly, truth-instilling sight;
The chaplet-wreath they wear upon their brow
Proclaims to all their late accomplish'd vow.
Tears start, to see each placid, radiant head;
You ask no questions; think, and all is said.
The statesman, long inured to worldly ways,
For this recurring pageant heart-struck stays.
The wither'd Talleyrand revives to see
Our human nature fraught with mystery,
Moved in his deep and labyrinthine soul
To view the past, the future, and the whole.
His moisten'd eye, his hand held out to bless,
Proclaim his cunning vanquish'd by a dress;
For dress so pure, combined with radiant eyes,
Denotes what fluent to the tongue ne'er flies,

Of those at least who deep impressions fear
When some faint glimpse of Heaven demands a
    tear.
But if the passing straggler this can move,
Within the church what must the vision prove?
Those looks of youth to its devotions given,
Display to men, if aught can show them, Heaven.
In woman's beauty, pious, thoughtful, grave,
There lurks a secret that can guide and save.
For true Religion is not wholly free
From elements supplied by what we see.
It is a concrete, partly flesh, refined
By contact with its inmate, graceful mind—
That angel-guest which often makes it be
Harmonious with diffusive mystery.
So when such Beauty kneels devout to pray,
Ah! then the shades of mind all pass away.
And then, within the church, where'er we turn,
What's heard and seen can make the bosom
    burn.
That Prelate's face in which you seem to see
Of eighteen centuries the history—
Augustine, Ambrose, Irenæus old,
Yes, Paul and Peter humbly, simply stoled,
Extorts a burst of heart-struck deep amaze
To see how Christian grandeur simply stays—
To see how in a world distracted, vain,
The Church her antique glory can maintain.
That face is as a book in which you read
The past and present wonders of our creed.

" *Strange matters* " truly to the thoughtful eye,
Which can through them the unseen world descry.
Oh! here, indeed, we need not words expend
To prove the Supernatural our friend.
That sight reveals this truth, and ever must
While Pride sinks humbly owning itself dust.
Enough; this vision high at length has ceased;
And now for action Innocence released
Prepares, by other rites exalting life,
To gird its loins, and wait the coming strife.
For now another wonder comes in view,
And such as the ancient world never knew.
Instruction is to all imparted high,
For which e'en sages had of yore to sigh;
A wondrous doctrine, practical and pure
Ope's mystic springs of action ever sure.
With this prepared, the rite its seal imparts
To strengthen and confirm soft youthful hearts;
The blow symbolic bids them all prepare
To combat nobly, and till death to dare.
The Christian duly form'd then takes his way,
Divinely armèd for the mortal fray.
Before him stretches now the world so wide,
The Supernatural his surest guide.
The mind, without it, undecided grown,
Contracts a painful, solitary tone;
For not to feel a will for that or this
Is just the *Me* within somehow to miss;
All indecision leaves us in this state
Of inward loneliness which we must hate.

The Supernatural, we know at length,
To our own will imparts a vital strength;
No longer absent from yourself, you can
Assert the native dignity of man.

So though through deserts dangerous and wild
We see now wander the oft puzzled child,
Still, found in Real Presence ever near,
The God who loves and saves him will appear;
Of strength, of goodness a perennial source
To every spring of virtue yielding force.
Controll'd by reason's ever steady voice,
Excluding all excess, eccentric choice,
This fountain might be call'd, from joy and youth
Supplying springs to one, to both their truth,
To nourish all the lofty and profound,
Causing to bloom what decks the lowest ground,
Whatever to humanity belongs
When made the theme of high Pindaric songs.

Or still the Supernatural attends
Him who through Nature's bowers ever wends.
Unseen it soars above the lover's way,
Exalting feelings with its potent sway,
He hears the movement of its mighty wing,
Which winnows round him in a mystic ring.
Of frost and senselessness unskill'd to boast,
'Tis he perhaps who feels these truths the most,
As Octave Feuillet so well displays
In tales as soft as our Shakspearian Lays.

Woman and man, when bound in equal love,
Have many thoughts that soar and rest above.
Each something hears, as in the primal times,
Which with true miracles symphonious chimes.
No lover true to Nature lone is left
As if of this great influence bereft;
But him through all his thoughts it will control,
He soon discovers that he loves a soul.
Bodies may die, not so transfigured love,
Which mounts o'er passion to the spheres above.
So this world fading, he recovers rest;
He yet can woo in regions of the blest.

Then all men find through life's entangled ground,
Where'er they turn, that miracles abound.
For all roads here below are found to be
Leading still onwards, while mysteriously
Far in the unapparent lies an end
For which the thoughtless even efforts spend.
The higher mankind mounts upon the scale
Of civilized existence, will prevail
Less satisfaction, greater discontent
As to the lot of each, however bent.
The Supernatural alone is found
To yield the remedy both sure and sound,
As lately was proclaim'd by French Le Play,
The independent statist of our day [7],

[7] La Réform Sociale en France. Paris, 1846.

F

Whose life to social problems has been given,
And who to solve them this way has been driven.
Then population, like each single mind,
In acts religious miracles will find.
For virtues supernatural acquired
Must needs be witness'd and in heart admired.
And this disposes of an argument
Which to exclude our line of thought is meant.
Belief in miracles some now assert
Must human rules of conduct all pervert;
The Supernatural, which we descry,
They say must thoughts and actions falsify.
Saints' intercession, prayer to Christ's own Mo-
      ther,
Must solid principles and conscience smother.
But they allude to some rhetoric cry,
Which sooth to hear proves often agony;
For men absurdly graceless in their mind
Of every cause as advocates you find;
In vile similitudes alone so strong
You wish that right on their tongues could be
      wrong.
The eloquence of schools with great pretence
Will often seem to outrage common sense,
By prompting pure extravagance with screams,
Ignoble accents of some studied dreams;
While calm and perfect Faith rejects such dress
Its deep and wise convictions to express.
But those who pray to Mary still are found
In action noble and in judgment sound.

Saint Bernard, or the lowest peasant here,
Methinks has not much cause this test to fear.
Then let these censors cease now to suspect;
Though that's the vein inherent in their sect.
Suspicion, trust me, is an odious guest
When once it enters any noble breast.
'Tis that which renders blind and falsifies
The judgment that still waits upon their eyes.
As when in pictures the perspective seems
To justify the fiery zealot's dreams.
Forgetting that the distant must show small,
However vast its greatness over all;
While what is near must needs be painted great,
Whatever be its minor lower state.
But this is parenthetical, and we
Return to virtues which the crowd must see
In those directed by this line of thought,
And must admire, when before them brought.
The pagan standard offer'd to their eyes
No longer dazzles, or yet satisfies.
They learn each moment what is needed more,
By instinct led to use the Christian store.
For Instinct, as in pagans from the first,
Conjoins with Reason there to quench its thirst.
In vain you would confine men to the field
Which only Nature's florets pale can yield.
While Humboldt to his latest hour defied
The Supernatural which he denied,
He wish'd, he said, he were not in his skin,
Such evening sadness reign'd, he own'd, within.

So after ninety years of life on earth,
To thoughts like these it only could give birth,
Instead of setting like the glorious sun,
So bright and gorgeous with its glad course run,
In purple radiance sinking to the sea
To recommence as through infinity
The placid labours of its beaming way,
To close alone where light will ever stay!
From such examples, now so fearful, stern,
The human heart will sweeter courses learn.
The vague sad mists of such philosophy
Will never cheer its void or satisfy.
The sun once risen, men will feel its beams
Pursue the real and forsake what seems.
The dreams of genius, passionate and bright,
Are thus enacted before human sight,
As true reality ; our life, entwined
With peace and hope, can its supreme good find.
For here, in short, both friends and lovers know
That joy above awaits the joy below.

And then, too, some reflect how this was known
To the ancestral races that we own.
Celts, Picts, and Anglo-Saxons, in their day
Pursued, like us, the superhuman way.
The Mediæval English, merry, free,
Revered this sphere of thought the same as we.
Their lowly youths and maidens so obscure
Had seen the churches which with us endure.

The tombs and monuments that still appear,
To them like home familiar were and dear.
Just as the hills, and dales, and tracks around
Recall'd the place where friends and joys were
    found.
With all were bound associations soft;
With Love's own whispers they were mingled
    oft.
All knew the spot where the old saint had
    knelt;
The truth that made him dear all likewise felt.
So thus the Supernatural unites
The youth of all times by the very sites
Which it ennobles, and can still impart
The self-same feelings of a docile heart.
The young of old, as all things clearly tell,
Were just like these whose hearts we know so
    well.
Quite simple, reverential, loving mirth,
With true affection for both heaven and earth.
Race after race with sentiments the same
Add fresh attraction to the holy flame.
For who would not resemble that past youth
In sweet submission to the voice of Truth,
Described by Chaucer's and by Shakspeare's pen,
Crown'd oft by angels when not sung by men?
Who would prefer to join the sophist's crew
That sought to mould humanity anew?—
The Past reduced to sheer annihilation;
The Future blank, a dark, cold isolation;

The Present but a riddle unexplain'd ;
For, after all, the mystery remain'd !

Distrusts and phantoms passing thus away,
Clear radiance lights up all with cheerful day.
At least on one road few will e'er disdain
To use what can a happy life sustain—
That life domestic with its graces high
Which sceptics even cannot quite deny.
Yes, there they own that far surpass'd is all
By that which Supernatural we call.
Self-love is quick to find out rest and peace ;
And thenceforth Reason may its lessons cease.

But yet there still remains a passage stern
Where most of all these truths men can discern.
For what surpasses nature when we die,
With greatest wonder strikes the human eye.
Now evidences on that path abound,
Their strength conclusive and their tenour sound,
To prove that nature unassisted, lone,
Could never realize that secret tone
Which sheds a foretaste, through a mystic scroll
By Faith, of union with the wondrous whole
Of central love that bathes in rapture deep
Beyond all poet's dreams in balmy sleep.
Then full of wonder, full of hope they part,
Just as a traveller at dawn would start.
Rupertus of Saint Gall, of wisdom meek,   [seek.
Call'd Deaths "*Excursions*," where we pleasure

Perhaps this sounds to some but as a whim;
Yet Death, indeed, seems not like Death in him.
Our Jane and Mary Anne did this way die—
A scene unearthly to the human eye!
A sight which future time can never blot
In those who saw it—ne'er to be forgot—
Theme not for words; but music's lofty sound
Alone should pass where thoughts are speechless
    found.
So Death grows Supernatural as well;
And this concludes the wonders that we tell.

What now remains ere we forsake the strain,
But with quick touches, briefly once again
To let some flashes of the mighty whole
Pour their bright radiance on the charmèd soul.
Thus Science, Reason, first came to our aid;
And now can poets see what life is made
By faith, which in a higher sense imparts
The light that kindles and dissolves our hearts;
Restored to Eden and its blessed fields,
Each primal wonder now we find it yields,
A rapture high that waits upon each thought,
Extending further than we ever sought—
Wonder, amazement, as when all began
To render happy new-created man,
God found in presence mystical to stay
With him through all the mazes of his way,
And then in death to meet us at the goal,
While granting joy immortal to the soul,

Its fleshly garment glorified to be
With all its radiance for eternity.

Then parts of Nature ne'er invoke in vain;
But let us view her wide transcendent reign,
Thus bounded by no limits that we know,
Eternal, infinite, for us to show
When our distinctions all must disappear,
And one vast glory seen be ever near,
The Supernatural as Nature still
Found to exist alike by Sovereign Will.
Such is the blazon on the Standard old
Of which the triumphs still we can behold.
When faithful to this ancient Flag unfurl'd,
" Good sense will rule as master of the world,
And human life," if Bossuet you hear,
Whose eagle-eyes distinguish'd all things clear.
Far be from us the folly, then, to think
That this great Light begins for men to sink,
That super-earthly things involve a doubt,
That future times their falsehood may find out.
Those who say this are potent to disclose
Some wondrous secrets which their science knows;
Inventions for destruction they can show;
What makes men happy they pretend to know;
But moral secrets of our inmost life
Present a field that has not seen their strife.
Say, whom amongst them can they ever find
To prove Augustine or Aquinas blind?

Saint Bernard, Richard, Pascal, claim a place
Where genius later has not left a trace.
Compared with these, we busy triflers seem,
Our labour vanity, our fame a dream.
Trust us you may in things material, small ;
But Christian sages soar abovè us all.

Then heed we henceforth never to repel
The guides who lead us to where all is well ;
The Possible respecting, when we hear
Of what is Supernatural and near.
That reign of which in truth we nothing know,
From which we issued, and to which we go—
The same for all conditions, ages, states,
Which gave us life, AND NOW WHICH FOR US
    WAITS.

Attentive, serious, be this then our part ;
While higher still we seek to raise our heart ;
To join in the great chorus there above,
The chant immortal of Eternal Love.

FAITH WITH NATURE.

SOME leaves that flit so playfully
Come down from hoar antiquity.
The Oak, methinks, might represent
The ancient Faith when age is meant.

It has its annals, legends old,
Such as are still at Cowthorpe told ;
Then sometimes a sepulchral tree
It haunted stands, a mystery—
As that in which the fell Glendower
Long hid the victim in his power.
A grave memorial of the past,
From Saxon times this oak will last.
Successive generations die ;
While he stands firm, majestic, by.
The Willow weeps, the Aspen croaks,
But we might call these "*talking oaks*,"
With more than old Dodona's power,
To sanctify our summer bower.
But though so ancient and so grave,
To stand alone each will not crave ;
Unlike the Pine, where all the ground,
Beneath it stripp'd, is naked found,
This patriarch, of Beauty friend,
Has no such jealous, hurtful end,
No leaves destructive round him spread ;
No verdure blighted, floret dead ;
As if he thought with constant toil
To stand sole tenant of the soil.
In these respects a type he stands
Of Faith throughout all times and lands,
Which now I seek to praise, admire,
While changing notes upon my lyre.

When Faith lights up the heart
Must Nature all depart,
A stealthy, branded culprit, loving night,
Who dreads a lightsome way
Where Truth can shed its ray,
And with its sweet dawn must commence her
flight,
As if, by instinct led, she knows
That He who is the Truth and she are ever
foes?

An enemy thus nigh,
Must Nature hide and fly,
As if she heard behind her, in the dark,
A step that follow'd still,
Which boded her but ill,
While bearing on her front a branded mark,
That all who meet her thus should know
To her no friendship sweet can Heaven's adherents
show?

Is Faith the true and old
So pale and deadly cold,
That lonesome she can only live, and grow
Where nothing else is found
To cheer and deck the ground,
Like Alpine floret on the barren snow,
Where man can scarcely breathe the air
That is so far above what he must love as fair?

Oh, no ! the heart replies ;
It is not Nature flies
When the great sun of truth bursts forth to
    shine,
To ope each beauteous flower
With a mysterious power,
And kindling hearts most delicate and fine
With joy that makes them feel and know
'Tis her blest beams that make all good and
    beauty grow.

Not pinnacled in clouds,
Midst peaks in frozen shrouds,
In cold sublimity she dwells alone ;
In tender hearts and soft
While raising them aloft,
She finds what can for humble things atone—
Affection clothing with its might
The fair and heavenly forms Faith brings to
    mental sight.

We see in one combined
All that are fair and kind,
All those still loved on earth or pass'd away ;
Yes, even trees and flowers,
The hues of summer bowers,
Seem all in one bright smile to sport and play,
While hearts the weakest, such as mine,
Around that radiance there alike will intertwine.

Our earthly Loves, still fair,
Will soar to domes of air ;
Not lonely, cold, bereft of friends we fly ;
In boundless regions vast
We find again the past
And present join'd as nurselings of the sky ;
What's loved on earth clings to our side ;
Not Faith like this entire will them and us divide.

Oh ! true the first great cure
For human minds and sure
Consists in sole unmix'd Divinity ;
But Nature, like a maid,
To follow like a shade,
May be proposed to wait in privacy
On her, and many things suggest
Which the great Mistress then will sanction as the
    best.

So thenceforth one for ever,
Faith wills not men should sever
The links that round our nature she has thrown,
For earth is needed still,
Combined with potent will,
To form that which God will not disown—
The man with feelings as first made,
Enabled now in faith to haunt Elysian shade.

Thus taught, to him appears
What to his heart endears
The life of Christ which pass'd upon this
earth—
The Child, the Boy, the Mother,
The Friend, Apostle, Brother,
Each fond relation from that mystic birth,
As when the Jews adoring knelt,
And still for all they saw both love and wonder
felt.

Then she, the Virgin blest,
In whom He took His rest,
Is seen as when she held Him in her arms;
The Christ and Mary dear
Together will appear
So closely knit in love that shields from harms;
For Nature simple feels no wrong
When both are loved and praised in one pure holy
song.

Then let the strain ascend
To where all wishes tend,
Let music's thrilling sound uplift the soul;
When to them both we kneel,
And tell them all we feel,
Of Faith and Nature, then we keep the whole,
Nor need we fear that He will be
Displeased as if such love should cause Him
jealousy.

His Godhead aye to trust
'Tis this He will'd from first ;
And what can prove that faith more strong and
pure,
Than when a Hebrew maid
Is now the Mother made
Of all, so long as time and men endure,
To whom as such we stedfast pray
That smiles from her may waft us to God's endless
day.

But lift your eyes on high,
Behold the altar nigh,
Where, in a frame of marble white as snow,
Murillo's Virgin stands
Upraised by Angels' hands,
As in a Nantuan church [8] we see her so.
Such beauty, pure, unearthly, mild,
To truth and Heaven belongs ; no ! not to man
beguiled.

Then hark ! the heavenly sound
Transporting all around,
Virgin, Mother, honour'd, and loved beyond
What any words express,
Till clothed in mystic dress
They utter symbols holy to respond

[8] Chapel of the Blessed Virgin, in the church of St. Louis,
at Nantes.

To thoughts that wing'd so upwards fly,
And are enroll'd above that they may never die.

Love breathes each word we hear,
And what to hearts are dear,
As Mother amiable and wondrous both,
As Maid of prudent mind,
Most clement and most kind,
While potent to resist the spells of sloth,
And faithful as a Mirror bright,
In whom all justice true and wisdom are in sight.

Then cause of all our joy,
With whom each heart can toy,
And scent the fragrance of a mystic rose;
We hear her named a Tower,
Davidic ivory bower,
Hung round with all the shields that Faith
bestows,
Gold house or Ark in which we trace
The seat vouchsafed to man for God's supernal
grace.

Yea, Gate of bright Heaven far,
Or sweet pale Morning Star,
Or her who tends the sick, for whom we sigh,
Who on our darkness smiles,
On each in sorrow's wiles,
Or who to help all Christians seeks on high;

Love, sin, grief, manhood voiceless grown,
Weep as if all were sung for them and them alone.

So on our knees we fall,
And feel the rapture all
Of one vast, boundless, comprehensive whole ;
In mystic vision bright
High Heaven brought to our sight,
The flesh itself ennobled with the soul,
Men feel as they would feel above,
Though tears below will steal from human eyes
that love.

Ah ! well to her we bow
Who did achieve the vow
Of Angels, Patriarchs, and Prophets old,
Apostles, Martyrs, all
Whom death did not appal,
Confessors, Virgins, and, what can't be told,—
The number infinite of those
Who to love God and life with Him immortal
chose.

Who seeks to "*deify*"
A creature in the sky ?
Avaunt the charge abhorred ! which nought
avails.
Do you forget the text,
With which none are perplex'd,
That seems to hush the wind before your sails,

G

Declaring men are Gods below
Who, all divine in thoughts, harmonious, orb-like
  grow?

   For God's sublime descent
   Implied man's strange ascent,
  Partaking of Humanity Divine;
    So when you Christians blame,
    And deem it to their shame
  That Mary in the heavens now should shine,
They own they do still more exceed;
So far are all your thoughts from their mysterious
  creed.

   Still say, ye pedants stern,
   Must we such prayers unlearn
  As not religion in its utmost height?
    Then call it what you will;
    Be this our tribute still;
  The heart proclaims that all is well and right;
It is what human nature brings,
Its purest gift to Faith, from which all goodness
  springs.

   Esteem it as you will;
   The whole is colour'd still

With hues that doubtless must to Heaven
  belong,
    With reason ever fed,
    To no good feeling dead,
It prompts at least an inoffensive song,
Not more forbidden than the strain
In which the world will chant its pleasure and its
  pain.

    Yes, call it but our way,
    When thus we sing and pray;
'Tis not religion; no, of course: no, no;
    But then what can there be,
    That man can hear or see,
More like that mystic action which we know
Than thus to sing, and praying fall,
Remembering her who bore the Christ who loved
  us all.

    Ah! you would have us be
    Reserved, discreet, that we
To no " *excess* " might ever be inclined,
    And sober above all;
    And this is what you call
To have a close reform'd to your mind;
No flowers, perfumed air, or fruit,
Crepuscular, dim souls and drear would ever suit.

    But "hearts fly to the head;
    Intoxication dread!
G 2

The Beautiful can give hallucinations [9];"
    When you have walk'd on stars,
    For you there are no bars,
No prudence, limits, and no Reformations;
The Empyrean, once thus drank,
For losing sober sense you have that cup to thank.

    Lo! shocking is your fall!
    Intemperance 'tis all!
Oh, fie! when rose-trees now should count their
    flowers!
    The Spring be less profuse,
    Too many nests for use
Of birds who must not sing so in their bowers,
When the sage Order of the Day
Demands much fewer stars to form the milky way.

    Deep truth is imageless,
    We know it and confess;
But there are other secrets to befriend,
    If we consent to see
    That our humanity
In Him alone achieves its final end,
Who visibly came from above
To cheer our flesh and sight with traces of His
    love?

[9] From the French.

This tribute then we say
Is what we all would pay,
Could we still see the Mother and the Son,
As when with love and awe
The first disciples saw
Her through whose Child high heaven might be
won,
Which the grave Magi too had felt
When low adoring there at feet of both they knelt.

Yes, say it now were told
That her you could behold
In some dark grot where poorest people stay,
What palace would compare
To the attractions there;
Or would the millions seek another way,
Though all that's glorious to the sight—
Great heroes, sages, kings, should elsewhere them
invite?

Our people too would bow,
Could they but see her now;
The youths that throng our streets would round
her play;
Their angel faces dear
Would feel the trickling tear,
And we, become as one, should wish to stay,
Dissent, and difference disdain,
To join united hearts in one sweet mystic strain.

Then let affection pure
For us this sight procure ;
In mind and heart that mother can be found,
A mother to our race,
Aye with us face to face,
Fann'd with the plumes of Angels kneeling
round ;
And English hearts will not be cold
To sing their artless hymns as in the days of old.

Loretto's song is sweet,
To utter love most meet ;
The words, though drawn from Scripture's
deepest lore,
Seem but like children's play,
Gathering flowers in May,
Each still fairer than what was cull'd before,
When cries of artless joy so bland
Denote that more is there than they can under-
stand.

Than this no sweeter flower
E'er grew in earthly bower ;
And if the heart must rise to heaven above,
Its grace descends to greet
These offerings so meet,
The beams of pure although a human love,
Lost in effulgence of that fire
Which Faith bestows on man all goodness to
inspire.

'Tis music of the sky
When thus we sing and cry;
It is to bask in smiles all joy above,
To float through domes of air,
To leave the earth, and dare
Enjoy the waves of deepest rest and love;
The breath of that eternal Day
Where Joy, and morning air, and Love for ever
stay.

SYMBOLIC GREETING.

WHAT harmonies gracious exist all around
To bind those who love men together!
These wreaths of Elysium can daily be found
Like bloom that we cull on the heather—

In feelings so similar, language as well,
In phrases so quaint used by all,
In looks and in gestures which each heart can
tell,
In homely things pleasant we call,

In fashions of dress closely followed by each
In the sense of what's right and fair,
In customs which all so familiarly teach,
The common surpasses the rare,

In the tints and sounds that we all of us love,
　　In fun, which no presence can smother,
Which seem to denote the same country above,
　　As if we all came from one Mother.

　　　'

And yet, as if Nature alone were deprived
　　Of such links to enchain our race,
Religion will offer what all has survived
　　When no one these signals would trace.

Oh, blossoms of silk of the soft willows tall!
　　Oh, the box and the yew-tree green!
How beauteous are ye when symbolical all
　　In the spring-tide in cities seen!

Uplifted by youth in our yearly grave rite
　　As palms of Jerusalem high,
As yielding a triumph in fancy so bright
　　Unto Him who comes there to die!

At present your stems only droop o'er the pool,
　　But Remembrance brings back the rest;
Though scatter'd your leaves on the waters grown
　　　cool,
　　The type still ennobles your nest.

Then here are the portals still open for prayer,
　　And now 'tis the sweet Vesper hour;
And lo! some young strangers stand all joyous
　　　there,
　　With faces that smile like the flower.

They pass in before you so blithe and so gay,
　　And then, what can yield you surprise,
The last turns smiling his homage to pay
　　With friendly and loving-glad eyes.

His finger just touch'd in the sanctified wave,
　　He stretches to join it to yours;
And you feel that an earnest of love he gave
　　Which wishes you joy that endures.

Whence come you, fair youth, now? from France
　　　or from Spain?
　　So versed in the thoughts of our heart,
Unknown to our eyes, ne'er to meet us again,
　　When here at this spot we shall part?

I think what a fountain of union is here,
　　For both a symbolic supply
Of that which from all alike drives away fear,
　　And promises life in the sky!

Where hands that once touched thus on earth's
    rugged shore
  May be joined in the angels' ring
In union for ever, and no parting more
  Such a vague, voiceless want to bring!

For here we soon parted ; 'twas only a glance
  Instantaneous, and each was gone ;
Oh! conjoin'd may we meet in the endless dance,
  Where we all are in bliss but one!

Oh! young foreign stranger, our thanks then to
    thee
  For using this symbol of love ;
And if this brief sign prove a rapture to see,
  Ah! what will it be there above

To find the thing signified shown to the soul—
  The endless and infinite won ;
The love that we dream of embracing the whole,
  Only shadows and figures gone ?

HONOUR OAK.

A THOUGHT that is familiar, trite,
Though grave, may cast a soothing light.
These leaves that will grow pale and flutter
Have no grim sounds that I would utter.
When once snapp'd off—away they fly—
Then what great evil so to die?
And even when they're fallen all,
There's nothing still should us appal.
They lie, 'tis true, upon the bank
To which they flew and downwards sank;
But even thus spread on the ground,
They nourish life in roots around.
Beware then how you touch their heap,
To hide them all away and sweep;
They rest in wise provision kind
That you may later others find
Just bright, and fresh, and green as they,
While lasted their sweet summer's day,
Imbibing from their substance still
What Nature's objects best fulfil;
Just as we hope when we are fled
And fallen this way, resting spread,
Some influence that's good may be
From our poor faultful memory.

So now discarding servile fears
Of what too trite to some appears,
Let us just mark how swiftly dance
The leaves as they to death advance.
And then from parks and gardens fair
To human graves we can repair
In thought, without abrupt transition,
Serenely calm, yet with precision,
Weighing the things quite unseen made,
When what was seen becomes a shade.

A busy life I know can please,
Compatible with mental ease ;
But fuss, and airs, and self-esteem,
Will strike me as a sickly dream.

I pass'd at evening by a hill
Where many dead lay lonely, still.
I wish you could have seen the spot,
So graceful ne'er to be forgot.
A blissful peace seem'd shed around,
That made me wish to kiss the ground.
I do not Fancy here invoke ;
The place is now call'd Honour Oak.
The many lay together near,
While some few stragglers did appear,
As if each chose some special spot
Though dreading ill reception not.
In death united there they lay,
Henceforth no evil part to play.

Methought I here had found the type
Of human nature, and would wipe
From my remembrance all the store
Of what had troubled me before.
Not here, as oft in life, we find
The pride, the jealousy unkind,
With which so pompously we greet
Each comer new we chance to meet—
Wrath-kindled gentlemen though sage,
Who easily are moved to rage.
Could we suppose that in the grave
The same old passions yet would rave
Hard-featured, proud, and angry looks
Be found, as oft described in books,
The false salute, the filmy eye,
When Generosity stood by ;
The cold, staid gait, and hollow smiles,
Or word which innocence beguiles.
With those foul marks which often can
Make hideous, vile, the living man—
That here, as in some public stand,
All would but utter gruff command ;
That each, though to his nook confined,
Against his neighbour jests design'd ;
Or oft would seem to eye the other,
All Nature's homeliness to smother—
That here the "*Reverences three*"
Of Goethe none did ever see—
I mean to what's above, around,
Beneath them, reverence profound—

That here, as in our Senate old,
Were passions more than could be told ;
That all would bargain and deceive
As well as did the serpent Eve,
As in the scene so many know
Between Panurge and Dindenault,
That, to evasive meanings bound,
Their talk was nothings of much sound ;
That here were but the crabbed old,
Pale with the quenchless thirst of gold,
Disdaining still the morning's smile,
The noontide basking for a while,
That blue divine, the evening's glow,
The greenwood-tree, the streams that flow,
That pleasure here for each would be
Some daily rich Gourmanderie,
Such as old Athenæus sings,
For dinner-loving Persian kings—
In short, that here, with none to blame,
All good was but an empty name,
Pure love and honour a mere jest,
As not of cleverness a test—
The only power to compete
With wealth that does their wishes meet—
Could we, I say, all this divine,
No peace upon these graves would shine.

But somehow an instinctive dread
Recoils from viewing thus the dead ;

And few on tombs would wish to show
Realities of life below;
Plantagenets themselves must lie
With hands uplifted to the sky;
And where the lark now mounts and sings
We find no trace of vulgar things.
We think that all now here are changed,
From evil nature quite estranged;
The ugly artificial face
Here, we imagine, leaves no trace,
As if had fallen off foul disguise,
Which just before had pain'd our eyes.
We fancy all low stretch'd out here,
Like the sweet youthful must appear,
Brave, kind, and faithful, loving still
Each that would now approach their hill;
Quite anxious to salute each brother,
As if they own'd one common Mother,
And just like those we think the best
Before they reach their final rest—
No fussy air, with selfish pride
To spread discomfort far and wide,
But sweet contentment, rest, and ease,
Their wish another still to please,
Preferring simply what's their own
To all the wealth by others shown.

But let me now the moral draw
From what I felt and what I saw.

Why then should not the living be
Just like the dead we think we see?
Why nourish anger's stupid strife,
To make a tragedy of life,
Or rather an ignoble play
At which buffoons alone would stay?
Forsaking Nature, Christian truth,
With all the visions high of youth,
With all the sweets to mortals given
When they will make existence Heaven!

Let all men hate the stupid rage
Which fires maturity and age,
Contracting habits selfish, mean,
Such as in youth are seldom seen,
Tones, looks, and ways from which we turn
While feeling indignation burn,
Almost a deep scorn for our race,
Which thus its nature can deface.
Let all be like the lowly, free,
The best type of humanity;
Humble and careless, blithe and glad,
With no false cares to make them sad.
Not with that movement infinite
Observed in things of smallest might—
Creatures whose littleness will worry,
And seeming in an endless hurry
(Like men who never now can stay
In the old, quiet, thoughtful way,

In any spot), with restless wings
Some instinct their ambition stings.
Whose small vibrations if you count
Six hundred swell the strange amount
Each second, to amaze the wise,
Whom such activities surprise.
Let all the living court the Muse,
Who rest with thought will chiefly choose ;
In town or country let them spare
Some time for love and friendship there.
Let them in life be hearty, brave,
Such as we'd see them in the grave ;
Like toil, let something make amends
For want direct of highest ends ;
With which, alas ! I greatly fear
That some, if living, would appear.
It is Plutocracy alone
That we recoil from and disown ;
Though that a higher influence
Can e'en from toiling thus dispense.
Then life would prove a peaceful field,
And every beauteous flower yield.
With Love and Faith then wing'd, and Hope,
They'd fly while other men would grope,
Through barren ways, entangled, wild,
To find themselves at last beguiled.
Then each would be a child of song,
At least in heart, to dread no wrong.
'Tis then they would delusions fly,
And find it even bliss to die.

H

Their grave would then indeed have peace,
And all mere suppositions cease.

MEDIOCRITY IN WISHES [1].

WHAT little wants has Nature aye to be
Replete with joy and from dull sadness free!
These leaves, these florets, smiling in your view,
Will only ask from Heaven the morning dew,
Sunshine and showers, and a wholesome ground—
These granted, all they wish for has been found;
And men no less might have their bliss complete
If only culling what lies at their feet.
See poets, when with Hugo they demand
What should we do 'midst troubles in the land?
We, only just escaped, as you might say,
From the small cradle where we softly lay?
We who all live upon a little shade,
And, like the birds, with air are happy made?
Oh! wherefore now to such an angry sea
Should my soft nest of moss confided be?
See artists, how they ever beauty trace
In what lies common to the human race—
See children, who the briers, brambles haunt,
To find in berries what no riches grant;

---

[1] Translated from old French.

Little low bushes yielding such a store
Of pretty playthings that they ask no more.
See youth, so blest beneath the hawthorn shade,
A very Eden with its perfume made.
His wishes bounded by success in speed ;
No dark intricate questions will he heed ;
Whate'er you want, with hands and feet he'll try
To grant ; for him there ends Philosophy.
See how, for all who round our nature cling,
The falling leaves and autumn breeze can sing.
Yes, moderate wishes, tastes, will serve us all,
Though winds will sweep and trembling leaflets
　　fall.

Of wishes such as most men entertain,
That all but what are moderate are vain,
Is what the wisest of the ancients thought,
Who to their wisdom life's experience brought.
And Heaven such just petitions often grants,
Refusing those for which ambition pants.
For daily bread we all are taught to pray,
No more than this to wish for on our way.
Some pray for patience, find it in their need ;
Would prayer, think you, be heard with equal
　　speed
If asking for a chariot in the sky,
Ay, or for conquest o'er some neighbour nigh ?
Ask to be rich as Job, as Sampson strong ;
To leave, like Abraham, for ages long

Descendants; or, like Absalom, to be
Handsome, and then just calmly say to me,
Would you still answers favourable find?
It is a question, to speak all my mind.
Now on this theme I pray you let me play,
In half a jovial, half a serious way.

A village woodman lived in days of yore,
Long, long ago, historic times before.
No record, therefore, tells us of his name;
I much regret it, but can no one blame.
Old Elian says that he was Thracian bred;
But Agathias he was Samian said.
All one to me; I shun such vain disputes,
And only seek what gentle hearers suits.
By felling trees this rustic gain'd his life,
Supported cottage, children, dog, and wife.
When lo! it happen'd on a fatal day,
His axe he lost, and with it all his stay;
For with his axe he lived in honour high;
Without his axe, of hunger he must die.
Death six days later met him with his scythe,
Prepared to mow him down with ghastly writhe;
But then began this helpless threaten'd wight
To pray to Jupiter with all his might,
Crying, praying, and with great learning too;
For need, you know, finds eloquence to sue.
His face uplifted, knees upon the ground,
His arms aloft, his fingers spread around,

Unwearied, crying, "Jupiter, my axe!
My axe! my axe! which timber ever hacks,
Oh! nothing but my axe, O Jove, or pence
Of a new tool to grant me the expense."
Now at this moment, in a council high,
Great Jove presided all abuse to spy.
Affairs were urgent; but this piercing voice
Did leave him then in fact no other choice
But to exclaim in council of the gods,
With frowns enhanced by awe-creating nods,
" What devil cries so horribly down there,
As if to hear him moments we could spare?
While things important, Virtue of the Styx!
Must here our whole attention constant fix.
What long prostrations and what fresh demands!
While each decisive answers still demands,
Vengeance or aid in their extremity
They all require; I'm in perplexity;
Nor am I yet decided what to do,
While each and all continue thus to sue.
This one has money, ready, sterling gold,
The other to obtain it would be bold;
One has learning to make all current pass;
The other is no wiser than an ass;
The one loves good, the other is beloved;
Although from good I think him far removed;
The one is cunning, cautious as a fox;
The other barks and heeds no hostile knocks.
A categoric answer is required,
To be adored by some, by all admired.

What tragedies excited by these cries!
And yet to hear them all I find time flies.
Sooth, this grave pastime suiteth none of us;
And yet a stranger now makes all this fuss!
Do, Mercury, just look down there below,
Lest inconvenience fresh and grave should grow."
The god invoked, a trap-door made to rise,
Through which what passes on the earth he spies,
As in a ship the captain has a hole
Through which he sees and can command the
     whole.
The fact soon known; he makes his due report
As one inured to justice to resort.
" Truly," says Jove, " they treat us mighty well,
As if of axes lost we needs must tell!
Have we no other *facienda* now
Than to attend to his wild rustic row?
Yet mark me, still, the cause is just as great
As if of Milan he had lost the state.
His axe is like a kingdom to a king;
We must restore this abject valued thing.
Go to, go to, and let no more be said;
To see this quickly done thou now art sped;
But where were we just now, I beg to know,
When interrupted by these cries below?"
Then some would haggle and excite debate
About what axes meant, the small or great,
While Vulcan cut a caper in the air,
Through love, they said, of some one absent
     there.

" Be off," said Jupiter to Mercury,

" That all my orders be enacted see.

This crying rustic needst not thou to greet,

But place three axes quickly at his feet ;

His own, another golden, and a third

Of silver.   Listen to what then is heard.

If he takes up his own and is content,

Say that to him the other two are sent ;

But if, quite dazzled, he will that disown,

Cut off his dead directly with his own.

Let henceforth all who lose their axes cry,

Be this their answer and their remedy."

These words pronounced, then Jove to all assem-
bled

Did make a face at which Olympus trembled.

Poor Mercury descended like a shot,

No item of his charge to be forgot ;

With wings expanded soon he clove the air,

And found the rustic crying, praying there.

Down at his feet he let the axes fall,

But so as not to scare him or appal.

" Enough hast cried," he said to him, " I think,

To need at last refreshment by a drink.

Thy   prayers   are   heard.   Behold   these   axes
three.

Now take thine own, and give the rest to me."

The rustic takes the axe of gold, and finds

Its weight excessive all his action binds.

" Upon my soul," he says, " this is not mine,

Although to you, indeed, it needs must shine.

Of this one silver I can say as much ;
Psha! bother these, I heed not axes such.
So take them both away ; but let me see
If this with wooden handle mine may be."
Then, seizing that, he spies an ancient mark ;
With joy he grows distracted, madden'd stark ;
Just as a fox that finds a straggling hen,
His transports secret knew no limits then.
" Leave me but this," he cries, " O dearest
    friend !
And a whole pot of milk to thee I'll send."
" Good man," the god replies, " now say no more ;
For choosing Mediocrity's rich store
In this here case of axes—take the rest ;
With all the three from Jove henceforth be
    blest."
The rustic thanks him, reveres Jove on high,
And then suspends his old axe on his thigh ;
The other two upon his shoulders bound,
He takes his homeward way, nor looks around,
Except to smile, or others eye askance,
As if some dreamer waken'd from a trance.
Have I, or have I not? he seems to say
To all who would accost him on the way.
The next day speeding to the nearest town,
For both the axes he was soon paid down
In ready money, with which then he bought
All that ever by richest lords is sought—
As sheep with the longest wool, and farms vast,
Meadows, vineyards, woods too that all surpass'd ;

Ponds, mills, and gardens, goats, and herds of
    swine,
Cows, oxen, calves, and all you wish were thine;
A grange, a hall, with quite a stately park,
To make all strangers passing by remark;
Horses, mules, asses, chickens, geese, and ducks,
Deer, both the fawn and red, with noble bucks;
While no new grandee in the country round
Has better crops and cultivated ground.
Such stiles of polish'd oak! Each gate, each
    fence,
Proclaim vast riches, and without pretence.
Old men would stare in groups and eye the rest,
Exclaiming, Riches, friends, alone are blest.
While no one in that neighbourhood before
Had of all household goods a richer store.

To charcoal-burners, all the country round,
To all the Smiths the news did quickly sound.
Deep envy soon disturb'd each wondering breast;
And no one from inquiring had rest;
So each must run and ask, and ask again,
Until he gets some information plain,
As to the means and place, and day and hour,
When he began to reap such wealth and power.
"What! what!" cried they, "and was the only
    cost
To have one day an axe like our one lost?
Is such, then, now the aspect of the skies,
The Ruling Planet which all else defies?

That who some little way his axe will pitch
Must suddenly wax powerful and rich?
Ha! ha! good axe, so now be lost you must;
I care not henceforth where you sink to rust."
Then, all their axes lost; most wretched he
To whom 'twas left his axe at home to see.
No son of a good mother then could tell
Where was his axe; no forest timber fell;
No wood was split through all the country wide,
For no one had his hatchet at his side.
'Tis said some little *gens-pille-hommes* who sold
Their mills to the late woodcutter for gold,
Now sold their swords, some axes to procure;
In order to be lost you may be sure.
So now began the chorus all around,
With each imploring that his axe be found.
All crying, praying, and lamenting then
To Jupiter, who grants such gifts to men.
"My axe! my axe!" each cried, "my axe, oh,
        dear!
My axe, great Jove, oh, cause it to appear."
The air resounded, as if tempest-toss'd,
With cries from those who had their axes lost.
Then Mercury three axes brought to each,
His own, one gold, one silver, to his reach;
When all, without exception, chose the gold;
And thanks to Jove were more than could be
        told;
But while each stoop'd, before his head could rise,
It falls, chopp'd off, and so each hero dies,

According to the edict of great Jove,
Which Mercury received up there above.
The number of the heads that these prayers cost
Just corresponded with the axes lost.

Oh, see then for yourselves what course to take;
For those who good prayers moderate will make
See the result, and henceforth understand
To shun excess whatever you demand.
No longer wish, as oft I hear you now,
For more than should be breathed in any vow.
For "Would to God," I hear you daily cry,
"That sixty millions in my bank did lie—
One hundred millions, all of sterling gold—
Oh, then my age would not feel weak and old!"
Experience tells you, when such words you spend,
That all in your discomfiture will end.
It is the scab, not fleeces, you will nurse,
Without one extra shilling in your purse.
Like those two lately, each a daring wight,
Who wish'd according to the Paris rite.
The one wish'd he might gain as much of gold
As had in Paris spent been, bought, and sold—
Ay, since its first foundation-stones were laid
Until the moment when his wish was made;
The whole esteem'd at highest value known
In dearest times from that age to his own.
Well, this one, think you, did he give a pledge
That unripe plums had set his teeth on edge?

The other wish'd the church of Nôtre Dame
From floor to roof with needles all to cram ;
And then to have of coins as many packs
As could be squeezed into as many sacks
As could be made with but one needle each,
Until they all had broken past the reach
Of art to make them serve that purpose more,
Not one point left to work with from the store.
Come, that is something like what we can call
Wishing, let happen still what may befall.

And what did happen, think you then, to each?
The shepherd's song-book quickly this can teach.
That very evening each of them then had
Upon his heel a scab contagious, bad,
A little cancer growing from his chin,
A cough denoting nought was sound within ;
Catarrh his husky throat did then assail,
And, last, an abscess formed on his tail.

Then only wish for what is moderate,
And never just desires overstate.
Let such be still your wish and prayer to Heaven ;
Then what you pray for will to you be given,
And greater things perhaps, if you but try
To labour humbly with calm industry.

Ay, but you say—The same it is to God
To grant directly with an easy nod

Some sixty thousand as the thirteenth part
Of what a shilling only will impart.
He is almighty, and can give the whôle
In gold as easily as one obole.
Ha, ha! and who has taught you, say, to speak,
You poor unknowing creatures, blind and weak,
Of God's Predestination?   Foolish man,
Peace! and be humble, wiser if you can.
Bow down now low before His sacred face,
And seek such lines of folly to efface.
Wait with but half an ounce of patience still.
Pray for what's just, and crown'd shall be your
    will.

THE OLD GIANTS.

LET others seek the hazel wood for prelude to
    their song,
When they would sound upon the harp what does
    to youth belong.
Oh! tell me not of nutting-days when you did
    fondly stray
On Norwood hill, and with a friend whose eyes
    were dawn of day.
I know that hazel foliage bright, in autumn rich
    like gold,
Is intertwined with merry tales that might to
    some be told,

That boys and squirrels there will rove at eve, and
    noon, and morn,
Digressing to'the purple fruit that grows upon the
    thorn.
But now the season fills the Park with children
    blithe and free ;
It is their pranks with dancing leaves that I would
    stop to see.
For lo ! with hoops leaves will contend in sportive
    mimic race,
And still rebounding, merry, light, will with their
    ball keep pace.
They fly, they flutter, rise again, they dance with
    grace and hop ;
They hasten for a moment on, and then the next
    they stop ;   [story ;
Well, all this is but infantine, a scene for fairy
Just let me then supply you now with ancient
    tales and hoary.
There's not a child amidst this band who has not
    heard the name
Of giants grim and dreadful once who could all
    tourists tame.   [whole,
Perhaps it might be very well to let them hear the
That they may know, with all their faults, these
    giants had a soul,   [day.
And often of a finer mould than pigmies of our
Do stop a moment, hear me sing, and mark what
    I've to say.

Of old the giants often err'd; not always justice
  wrought,
But often too they had a mind to suit true gentle
  thought.
Subjective still their painters were, and this ex-
  plains the whole,
While we pourtray some sly mean dwarf with dry
  and wither'd soul.
These painters might themselves be rude, imper-
  fect; it is sad;
But somehow still more feelings deep those gene-
  rations had.
Their giant is in fact themselves, no cunning, no
  disguise,
While saying, acting nobly oft to fill us with sur-
  prise.
A frail and giddy monster too, uncouth he will
  appear,   [tear.
But still within he has a heart, in eyes a starting
You laugh, declaim, invoke and rage, and call him
  monstrous rough,
But all the while you recognize in him heroic stuff.
His faults all open, wide, are there, protruding
  through his skin,
But still you can't prevent yourself from loving
  what's within.
Thus we read a giant young cites the tale by
  Plutarch told,
Of what was heard by Thamous, that pilot firm
  and bold—

How Thamous, while sailing on and near Palodes
    isle,   [mile,
Did hear a sound convulsing woods many a weary
Of voices wailing in the air, which cried to earth
    and skies,
That Pan, the great mysterious god, now at that
    moment dies—
How Cæsar, then Tiberias call'd, from hearing the
    report
Had sent for Thamous to come and tell it in his
    court—   [said
How, after hearing him, he believed, even loudly
The truth, not known to either then, that Pan
    (our all) was dead—
That Shepherd, not like Corydon, who loved alone
    the sheep,
But He who for the shepherd too would toil, and
    sigh, and weep ;
At whose departure the machine of this whole
    universe,
The course of sky, and earth, and sea, and hill,
    did all reverse.
And when the giant told it all to those who stood
    around,
He sat in silence, thoughtful still, with eyes upon
    the ground,
When tears as large as ostrich eggs were soon
    beheld by all
From his great eyes contemplative to trickle down
    and fall.

The pigmies whom we love to paint would tell it
    quite unmoved,
For from all depths of good and great we feel our-
    selves removed.
But this is merely prelude now to what I wish to
    sing,
Which, sooth, is but a trifle slight, a silly, childish
    thing.

This unnamed giant had for sire another far more
    great,
A tall youth, of whose early ways I somewhat
    would relate.
As yet a young and hopeful boy, who all his life
    will ride,
He first would wooden horses have, and keep them
    at his side.
They all must change their colour oft, just as in
    church we see
The vestments which with festivals must in their
    hues agree.
For lads like him, observers deep, in church will
    always find
Some gracious type of what is fair, accordant with
    their mind.
So skins, white, purple, red, and black, at times
    they all must wear,
Adjusted, fitting them so well, it seem'd their
    native hair.

I

What, purple! will you proudly cry.   Who ever
    yet did see

A horse so hued?   A trifle that; so still he'd let it
    be.

Besides, just enter Saint Sulpice, where Eugène
    De la Croix

Has painted such a steed to life, and it I lately
    saw.

Away with realistic views, they suit not giants
    well;

And let me simply now proceed of what remains
    to tell.

Well, sheep and calves, and otters too, supplied
    him at his need

With colours wherewith then he could his harm-
    less fancy feed.

He had a hunter made of oak, a roadster of a
    press,

A mule from an old bedstead carved, and these
    he'd ride and dress;

Relays besides he had some twelve, for service of
    the Post;

He loved them when he rode along, though when
    in bed the most;

For there they all must sleep with him, no other
    stables known;

Each too had still some special name, and they
    were all his own.

It chanced one day that there should come to see
 his father dear
The Lord of Painensac; when lo! two others did
 appear,
The Count of Mouillevent arrived with Duc de
 Francrepas ;   [Papa.
So many guests did puzzle much the servants of
For, sooth, the lodging was but scant, though
 stately, fine, and tall,
To hold such princes with their trains, the stables
 most of all.
The varlets of Lord Painensac began to look
 around
To spy if other stables void might not for them
 be found ;
When seeing my young giant knave they whis-
 per'd in his ear,
And ask'd if his great horses too had not their
 stabling near.
For men thus shrewd will always think that
 youths like him so gay
Will indicate, with winks at least, what others
 will not say.
He gravely leads them instantly to mount a terrace
 grand,   [stand.
Where did the lofty castle proud uplift itself and
Then through a hall and gallery they pass into a
 tower ;
At other steps to mount again, the groom stops
 short, looks sour.

"This boy but mocks us," he exclaims, "what
    say you?   Let us stop.   [top."
I never heard of stables yet placed at a house's
The other called his thoughts too quick; at Lyons
    he had seen,
At Barmette, and at Chisnon too, where stables
    such had been.
But still let's ask; "My little dear, pray, whither
    are we led?"
"To my great horse's stabling, sooth, all which
    you'd see, you said.
We shall be there immediately, so mount, and do
    not stand;"
Then neither longer would suspect the youth that
    look'd so bland.
Still passing by another hall, his bed-room door
    was next;
He open'd it, and said to them, who stood still
    more perplex'd,
"Here are the stables, and the steeds that you so
    wish'd to see,
Hungarian, Spanish, Flemish those, and this from
    Gascony.
That white one came from Francfort town, and
    him I'll give to you;
He suits me well, but all the same, and ain't he
    fair to view?   [back,
With half-a-dozen harriers, when mounted on his
You'll soon have hares and partridges to fill your
    daily sack."

"We *are* well off!" they both exclaim'd; they
    could not yet decide
Whether to laugh, or with pure shame themselves
    somewhere to hide.
Descending all confused, they heard, " A halter
    now would you ?"
"Oh, sooth!" they cried, "we've had enough; for
    this time that will do."
"I think you will be Pope some day." Said he,
    " That's what I mean ;"   [intervene.
" Exactly so," they said, "we think, whate'er may
God keep you from all evil, child; you have a
    guileless tongue,
But ready too, and, had we stopp'd, all changes
    you'd have rung."
While hasting down the staircase then their
    charger they let fall,   [appal.
Which did amaze the giant lad, and even half
" What horsemen ! oh, my stars !" he cried; "now
    say, had you to go   [know,
From here to Cahusac, and tell, that I may strictly
Whether you'd wish to ride a goose or lead a pig ?
    just think."
Replied the valet, "Neither, sooth; I would much
    rather drink."
Then finding their companions there, they told
    them all the tale,
Which made them laugh to split their sides while
    passing round their ale.

But I must strike another chord while you can
    still deplore
The way that giants' sons were bred in those past
    days of yore.
I grant they were not learned men; they often
    were perplex'd;
At many of your questions now they sorely would
    be vex'd.
'Tis true, when challenged to debate by a great
    English sage,
The giant student, all abash'd, did turn many a
    page
The day before and half the night, to find what he
    should say.
Vast volumes piled on every side, before, behind
    him, lay.
De inenarrabilibus Plotinus he must read,
De Numeris et Signis too, a folio grim, by Bede;
Peri Oneirocriticon Artemidorus gave,
Next came Peri Demeion, by Anaxagoras
    grave;
Deinarius Peri Aphaton would then perplex his
    brains,
Hipponax De Anecphoneton all his spirit drains.
But giant youths had always then an elbow friend
    at need,
Like one then saying books like these could only
    dulness breed.
Just drink a glass and then to bed, and leave the
    sage to me.

Without these thoughts immoderate I shall have
    victory.

That Englishman shall be reduced, and shortly
    " *ad metam*

Non loqui " be he e'er so learn'd, or I a donkey
    am.

" But oh! he is so deep," replied the giant,
    " dearest friend."

" Bother your deepness," cried the pal, " his fame
    will quickly end."

It is not this way young lads now escape examina-
    tions

Competitive; methinks I hear the pedant's ex-
    clamations.

Well, let them triumph, cram and pore, yes, pore
    and cram away;

'Tis but the folly of our times, the madness of
    a day.

I grant these giant youths were not proficients to
    divine,

Advise, select, distinguish, drink, the best and
    dearest wine.

A growing fear to meet with bad they thought
    would indicate

Somewhat rather of decline, of a setting in their
    state,

And that the noon for them was past; though
    boys with us refuse

To taste aught to the table brought but such as
    gourmands use.

Unlike the poet Alcman old, who hated dainty
    meat,
And all but that quite homely food which common
    people eat [2].
I grant these same tall lads were not as skill'd as
    many now;
That critics sharp they would avoid, and cared not
    greatly how.
Calphurnius Bassus wrote a book for some like
    them and me,
Whose hand-writing, uncouth and quaint, illegible
    might be;
He call'd it, too, De Literis Illegebilibus,
A study that I own might be of use to some of us.
But still, I think, each never proved a sorry archi-
    tect
Of consequences natural, who could no flaw de-
    tect.
'Tis known now by the microscope that insects
    possess eyes
With which the human vision clear by nature
    never vies.
On numbers infinite of points pertaining to de-
    tail,
Compared with these, our powers thus will prove
    of no avail;

[2] οὔ τι γὰρ οὐ τετυγμένον ἔσθει·
ἀλλὰ τὰ κοινὰ γάρ, ὥσπερ ὁ δᾶμος ζατεύει.
                      Athen. lib. x.

'Tis so with giants' synthesis, the dwarfs can see
    the specks
Especial with a sharpness keen that would their
    betters vex ;
But yet, 'tis the gigantic wights that see, and
    ever will,
Better than all the creeping ants of their mean
    little hill.
And how is man himself the lord of all we meet
    below ?
No masterpiece in any part on him did God
    bestow.   [excel.
Take but his skin; a tanner finds a rat will him
Surpass'd in eyes and muscles, ears, he is, and eke
    in smell.
He reigns but by the matchless whole of what in
    each division
Would prove to eagles, lions, owls, a matter for
    derision.
These giants too were simple, grand; the dwarfs
    are complicated ;
For littleness contrivance has, far more than can
    be stated ;   [by ;
The horse has not so many legs as beetles he runs
The cockchafer has twice the wings with which
    the eagles fly.
The one great, deep, high, intuition which the
    giants had,
Was better than the myriad dreams of dwarfs with
    doubting sad ;

Who, like Philetas, might complain upon their
 early tomb
That Reason false, and thought by night, for life
 had left no room [3].
These long-continued mortal cares from simple
 thought estranged,
But lead to movements which will soon be stopp'd
 or disarranged.
They signify deficiency, a rude and savage
 state,
Not that which our young giants knew, perfec-
 tion's latest date,
Accordant ever with the way that Nature all pre-
 pared,
Of complication needless first, until at length she
 dared
To rise to the conception skill'd of the great
 Simple, thus
Leaving it to these mortal fools to make an end-
 less fuss.
The giants' sons were often rude, but never sly
 and base ;
Of skill to cheat, deceive with tricks, you see in
 them no trace ;
That they left fathers, mothers dear, I find but
 little proof,
Renouncing all police restraints, obedience kept
 aloof,

---

[3] Athen. lib. ix.

Bound by secret league together, their "nation"
    for their God;
Prepared to scatter death and woe at some grim
    leader's nod,
Like dark conspiring felons, who for "*nationality*"
Declare with rage gigantic they Republicans will
    be;
Inflamed with ardour for a name, a fancy, or a
    word,
Although the thing implied should be irrational,
    absurd,
Diminutive in choice of themes, of objects to at-
    tain;
Yes, even when they might have cause with jus-
    tice to complain;
Renouncing the sweet visions high their land did
    once inspire,
That their wild, dark, ideal bond, Italians might
    admire;
Despising all antiquity, just order, right, and law,
Quite self-emancipated thus, them doubtless no one
    saw;
Disdaining, hating all their life, and calling them-
    selves free,
Because they loved and cherish'd subterraneous
    liberty.
That, weary ever of repose, in no place to re-
    main
Beyond a day was their decree, foretold in lan-
    guage plain,

We do not find, or that with them the sole autho-
        rity
Lay with those men who had no faith, or hope, or
        charity,
As in the deluge long foreseen and sung by poets
        old,
Who said that to the sophist's crew men's judg-
        ments would be sold;
When times would come when no one would resist
        their sottish voice,
But all would be as creeping things submissive to
        their choice;
When he who had the smallest heart, diminutive
        though proud,
The merest Liliputian, might be chosen by that
        crowd.

So running o'er the strings again, the prelude with
        the end,
In praises of *Philosophy* I'll leave you breath
        to spend.
We never can be well assured by reason, Science
        cries,
That we've attain'd the final limits of the smallest
        size;
The last degrees of littleness no instruments dis-
        play;
Of moral life, perhaps, as well we could the same
        thing say.

Give me the sons of giants, then, contented to be
    young ;
Take you the pigmy's children old, and now the
    whole is sung.

SOME GOOD IN ALL.

WHAT beauty pass we daily by
And nothing that is fair descry,
With whole unmitigated praise !
We only mark defective traits.
The beech-tree seem'd to Gilpin round,
Not by his views of beauty bound ;
So then he deem'd no names too hard
For what his theory had marr'd.
And thus would many censure here
Fair things that could most bright appear.
These leaves are not so fresh and green
As when in May they first were seen.
But yet their fibres and their hue
Have much to please, if only you
Attentively at each would look
Sly nestling in its quiet nook.
Through life I hold no one need tire
Observing grace he might admire.
Methinks the art of arts must be
To find what's good with charity.

A certain dog that no one own'd,
Accustom'd to be often stoned
By boys who mark'd his skulking gait,
As one inured to scoffs and hate,
Was caught one day within a ring
Of urchins, each of whom would fling
Some taunts as missiles at his head,
As he slunk here and there with dread.
They criticized each ugly part,
And still found new expressions smart
To raise a laugh, and justify
The unkind humour of their eye,
Until some maidens passing near
Felt pity; though to let appear
Their feelings they were half afraid,
Lest these rough lads should worse upbraid.
At last,—amidst the shouts and cries,
As tail, ear, nose, and legs each tries
To single out for general scorn,
Showing a wretch the vilest born,—
A sweet soft voice was heard to say,
Like music, to arrest the fray—
" You boys may keep on jeering so;
But yet his teeth are white as snow.
He may be plain—but what, then, pray,
Of all plain people will you say?"

The incident which here we find
Involves a trait of gentle mind;

SOME GOOD IN ALL. 127

For this poor cur experienced then
The treatment shown to absent men,
Where social circles take delight
In marking all defects with spite,
Where eyes and minds alone are clear
To watch and make our faults appear.
" Pray now observe," they say with pride,
" How vainly these we seek to hide.
Oh, what poor flimsy arts, and thin!
Who would be in such spotted skin?"
Nought they can spy that merits praise,
But only pure defective traits;
Some fresh fault each one sees arise,
Eliciting indignant cries;
Until some woman's voice is heard,
Unlike the tones of all that herd,
Exclaiming, " Well, but see the part
Which justly can no shame impart,
While you go on the rest to tell,
Here I must stop to mark what's well.
'Tis small, I grant, and oft conceal'd,
Most rarely to our eye revealed;
But this is sound unlike the rest;
At least let this for once be blest;
'Tis like the teeth of this poor cur;
To praise it do not then demur,
But own, for once, that even he
Has some faint claim on charity."

May such a voice one day be heard
When we're bespatter'd by the herd
Of those who think that all is well
Provided but the truth they tell.

THE DROWNING FLY.

IT is not we alone who feel
What stealthy time will soon reveal.
All life perceives mysterious change
That joy and calm will disarrange.
It is not only leaves that fall,
For insects hear the distant call ;
Some underneath the fading plant
Will vainly struggle with their want.
They drop from branches stain'd and bare,
As stiff with cold from alter'd air ;
They fall with the snapp'd broken bough,
Gardens seem growing deserts now ;
Shelter in nooks they creep to find,
But they're found out by shifting wind.
Some fall on pools and gasp for life ;
But short for them their earnest strife,
Glad yesterday on bright parterre—
Now plashes dark and death are there.

In little things, my friend, we see
Full oft a latent mystery—
Some tender touch of nature mild
To entertain a thoughtful child.
Let me a recent instance state
Which still perhaps can indicate
Things which in prose you never hear,
Though, sooth, to poets they are dear.

A silly fly the other day
Would, truant-like, take danger's way ;
On drinking milk was his intent,
Which, after all, was innocent.
Him gasping in a pool I found,
With no means left to reach the ground,
Till I, for him a mystic power,
Transferr'd him to a fairy bower,
As then to him it must have seem'd,
While still of nought but death he dream'd ;
Like in some ancient tales the knight
Who, from a dungeon dark as night,
Found himself once deliver'd free,
Brought back his own sweet home to see ;
So this poor, tiny, helpless fly,
Was thus preserved mysteriously.
Miraculously drawn to land,
He lay, poor wretch, but could not stand ;
And here the lesson grave begins
Which deeply my attention wins.

K

In cases such, I'd have you know
What, if you can, you should bestow.
Pile o'er him, then, some mounts of salt,
And he escapes from death's assault.
The mountain quivers at its head,
Convulsed by one you thought was dead.
The drown'd stark corpse begins to stir,
And then emerges with a whirr;
He opes his wings and takes his flight,
And passes quickly out of sight.
Or on absorbing paper placed,
As through a marsh his track is traced;
Imbibed, the water leaves him dry;
At least I've heard, and mean to try.
But I had no specific near,
And so there still was cause to fear.
For, weak and drench'd, half dead he lay,
His own poor efforts to assay.
But how he used them was the wonder
On which I now would have you ponder.
Recovering some little strength,
To cure himself he tried at length;
He scraped each wing; he smear'd it well
With what he had in secret cell;
He scraped till I grew somewhat tired,
Though patient art should be admired.
At last his process he would stop;
And then he found he could but hop.
His wings so glued could not expand
To bear him o'er the driest land.

He quickly fell, and, spinning round,
Produced a sharp and fitful sound.
But soon, this paroxysm o'er,
Determined he seem'd all the more.
With human practised skill he vied,
But falling still on either side,
The cure was so far incomplete;
His wings would not his wishes meet.
Yet hope survived; he tried again;
And sooth I felt for all his pain.
So now he took to rubbing more;
I think exhaustless was his store;
He scraped; he smear'd; once more he tried;
But all his science was defied.
This poor wing'd patient not downcast,
I thought he would succeed at last;
And so it proved; for in the end
His strength of pinions seem'd to mend;
Until at length he flew away,
And left me musing this to say—
That wantonly we should not slay
Our fellow-creatures of a day,
To whom is sweet this light and life,
Like us with dangers oft at strife.
What costs them thus laborious toil
We should not wish for play to spoil.
Superior beings, we can be
For them angelic ministry,
Or else a demoniac power
To work them evil in their bower.

K 2

Some deem it but a morbid sense
To pity flies—a mere pretence.
Though plumed they cut the golden air,
No insect such men ever spare.
Triumphant with their microscope
They would in living entrails grope,
Or amputating heads of flies,
While each his cruelty denies;
For since they are formed not like us,
They call us fools who make a fuss;
They cut, impale, they crush, enclose
In cement, scorning creatures' woes.
They'd fling them, laughing, in the fire,
And only your protests admire.
Lord Bacon praises vivisection,
And scouts poor Celsus's objection,
Thinks that all is well directed
When live beasts are thus dissected;
But his " necessity sublime"
Will seem to us quite simply crime.
For still the human heart, when sound,
Can make distinctions all around.
For man may use dominion just,
But not in power wholly trust.
The universe may have its plan,
A mystery as yet for man;
But that is no excuse for him
When cruelty becomes his whim.
The lesson you may deem but small;
With you I will not strive at all.

There is in man a sense profound,
Disdaining words and all their sound ;
And he will feel, whate'er you say,
That mercy is the safest way.
Call it but folly if he must,
To that, not science he will trust.
For sparing life he will not sigh
When his lone thoughts are deep and high ;
That needlessly he stopp'd no breath,
Will cause him no regrets in death.

INDEPENDENCE.

On paths through the forest we long since began
To doubt of the wisdom taught sometimes by man.
The woods teach dependence upon one another,
But men independence of father and mother.

See the branches and leaves so wide and so high ;
On them it is always that insects rely.
Species two thousand on the oak will depend ;
His foliage, and timber, and bark he must spend,

While paying the tax that these tribes will im-
    pose,
As every woodman and wayfarer knows.

Beetles and butterflies, moths small, gigantic,
All are his pensioners, some quite romantic,

Like Camberwell Beauty or Merveil du Jour,
Which all forest rovers so love to procure.
Then myriads of insects too live on the beech,
Whereby that fine handsome tree lessons will
    teach.

The ash a menagerie seems to support,
Such grim-titled moths to his keeping resort—
The Hawk, Goat, and Leopard, the Tiger as well,
These all have their residence snugly to dwell.

The old elms and willows, the larch and the fir,
Must creatures support, or there would be a stir!
While to parasite plants each often must bow,
As when crab-trees stretch out their mistletoe-
    bough.

The ivy alone, falsely class'd with that race,
Will still with great neighbours familiar keep
    pace,
Receiving its nourishment all from the ground,
It needs must embrace all the friendly trees round,

While asking no more than mechanic support,
And honestly feeding where it will resort.

Though connexions like this, so constant and dear,
End only when trees will themselves disappear.

Such then are the ways of the trees of the wood ;
But often with men these are not understood
As yielding a lesson important to each,
Which can mild contentment the generous teach.

Lo ! high Independence comes forth now to stalk ;
Through all the proud city there's nought like his
    talk,
So absolute, scornful, while looking around,
Though sure that there's no one can like him be
    found.

For nothing he owes to man, woman, or boy ;
And Debt is a word that he'll never employ,
Unless he can make out 'tis owing to him,
To suit his own proud and insatiable whim.

All virtue, according to his ceaseless saws,
Consists not in paying, but in what he draws
From others created, possessing their pelf
To serve but his own and ungenerous self.

The only wise head that can be upon earth
Is right proud, and the enemy sworn of mirth.

All others are honoured to be but his tools ;
And those contradicting he sets down as fools.

But now I would have you endeavour to try
Some quite debtless new world that suits him to
        spy ;
So let it be one Metrodorus conceived,
His thirtieth call it which you have received.

Well, then, amidst planets, it could but go wrong,
When, proud, to no others it still would belong.
No more of old order, but all disarranged,
The face of the universe instantly changed.

Old Saturn, Mercury, bright Venus and Mars,
Would feel perturbation, while each movement
        jars.
The moon left in darkness, the sun would no
        more
Dispense his rich light from his own ceaseless
        store.

Why, pray, should he shine on it or on earth's
        ground,
While free, independent, and to no world bound ?
No kind transmutation in elements then ;
When nothing was lent, say what owe they to
        men ?

No more debts to pay, since no power will lend ;
A kennel of dogs would the universe end. .
Then no man another would ever salute ;
To render assistance would nobody suit ;

Let them all cry out, help, fire, water, or death,
They might just as well have retained all their
    breath ;
For no one has lent aught ; so no one will pay,
No interest he feels then in all that you say.

In brief, from humanity banish'd would be
Faith, Hope, and, best of all, sweet, blest Charity.
But all men are born to succour each other ;
And if each his debts will thus cancel and
    smother,

Mistrust, and contempt, and wild anger remain ;
Maledictions and woes no life can sustain.
'Tis Pandora's bottle that then would be spilt,
A vast flood of misery nameless and guilt.

Bellerophons, Lycoons, Nebuchadonosors,
All are like robbers' sons, and men of no honour,
    sirs ;
Ill thinking, ill wishing, and bearing dark hate,
With each against all—such would then be their
    state.

Far easier much to keep fishes in air,
For stags under oceans to find their true lair,
Than for an hour to bear a world without debts ;
The thought of it irritates, horrifies, frets.

And now if each only his fancy employs
To dive within debtless man, he'll hear a noise,
Not, sooth, like a harmony moving the spheres,
As in the first glorious and still lasting years.

The head to the hands and the feet would not
      lend
Its eyes on their whims and vagaries to spend ;
The feet would not carry, the hands would not
      toil ;
The heart would be furious with all the turmoil

Of pulses through members that it would disown ;
And then for itself it would keep all its own.
Suppress'd would be each thing essential to life,
And that world so little would see only strife.

The brains, quite bewilder'd, would rave in the
      dark ;
The nerves would be motionless, muscles all stark.
In a world this way whirl'd and got off the rail,
Where lending and paying no longer prevail,

You'd see a conspiracy worse than was told
In fable, all figured by Æsop of old,
To perish, though wise Esculapius would try
That it should still hobble on while loth to die.

The body would putrify, and the poor soul,
Indignant, would fly to the devil's control.
So now, Independence, strut, pass on your way;
We heed not your vaunts, no, nor all that you say.

Such poor vapid boast ne'er from me shall be
    wrung;
We seek to be found mere dependents among.
From tops of high towers God often repels
Those in whose vain breasts Independence thus
    dwells.

But mossy nests humble, where many rejoice
To hear some sweet song by a soft gentle voice,
We know that He looks on with favour for ever;
So when shall we seek Independence? Why,
    never.

And even if Wisdom would still disagree
With all the old notions of Christians, so free,
Though Puritan manners should elsewhere pre-
    vail,
True Love will still whisper its own little tale.

You may cite exceptions; but such is his law,
Imposed upon all who his sweetness would draw,
If a heart you would conquer you must stoop low;
We cannot explain it, but still it is so.

Perhaps 'tis that servitude indicates youth;
I know not; but certainly it is the truth,
So long as a master we cherish and own.
What's sweetest and best cannot wholly have
    flown.

Avaunt! the grim pedants who liberty sing;
Give me a Master, and Love's light mounting wing;
An emblem in this of what soars above all,
For proud Independence preparing a fall—

Heaven's truth, which descended on earth from
    the sky
To teach man dependence and Pride to defy,
Showing what Master a mere servant became,
Our haughty impatience for ever to shame,

Though boasting as loud as Niagara's roar,
That Dependence can't breathe on Liberty's shore,
That patriots glorious were those who unfurl'd
The banner that makes independent the world.

THE STORM.

If calm, unruffled, still were Nature's face,
    Stern Cold's forerunners, slily hither sent,
Might welcomed be ; no mischief we should trace ;
    No leaf would fall, no flower's wand be bent ;

These envoys would arrive in such disguise,
    That they would be unknown to those they
        met ;
But let the winds of autumn once arise,
    Then follow scenes that you will not forget.

The coming season is with forces strong
    Provided—various in their dress and forms,—
A soundless air, rain, fogs, frost, all will throng ;
    But his first fierce advances are in storms.

Those of the Equinox quite unawares
    Arrive, unthreaten'd, take you by surprise ;
For them no leaf or flower bright prepares,
    Till, all at once, each flutters, breaks, and dies.

But distant echoes sometimes indicate
    A wild commotion in the clouds and under;
Then in great straits are flowers delicate,
    When peal on peal succeeds of clashing thunder.

For rapid fatal changes will take place;
    It is not now that storms can halcyons send;
'Tis summer's beauty that they will efface,
    While yielding proof that it draws near its end.

Then rain pours later with vast sheets of grey
    To cover gardens like one gloomy couch,
Dull drops still falling from each tender spray,
    Till clouds dispersing will a storm avouch.

Oh, hark! the groves so distant, how they sigh!
    Now nearer waves of atmosphere will swell;
The destined leaves all scatter'd now must fly;
    While moths and butterflies will seek some cell.

Straight on, resistless, passes now its Force;
    The flowers must hide, gigantic trunks will
        bend,
While in each corner, for a sly resource,
    The fiercest whirlwinds it now will send.

The birds have somewhere fled; no life is seen;
    The insects creep to crannies there to die;
'Tis the last act of what has lovely been;
    Hosts of leaves, routed, sweep across the sky.

Yet storms cause high scenes in the human life;
    Come witness now a purpose that they serve,
While watching, interested, the dreadful strife
    That from our object we may never swerve.

The storm it is that will find out the vile;
    'Tis he that smells and hunts the noxious
        game;
We can at least a moment well beguile,
    An instance citing that is full of shame.

Yes; storms, like other dangers, yield a test
    To ascertain what's hidden in the heart,
When even Piety will quit thy breast,
    To play the common rudest hero's part.

In Feuillet's tale, a theme for noble verse,
    The storm to Sybil thus reveals the saint.
Of that good curate mark now the reverse
    In one whom Rabelais did deftly paint.

To show how mortals often vainly rave,
    Concealing passions sly yet ever strong,
The formal hypocrites, the cowards brave—
    In comic verse, methinks, cannot be wrong.

Then let me sing a ship with merry friends,
    Who pass delighted o'er the ocean stream,
Until their bliss, thought sure, abruptly ends,
    A tempest rising worse than any dream.

Now suddenly the sea begins to rise
  From the dark depths of the unfathom'd brine ;
Their vessel seems to mount up to the skies ;
    The masts, and spars, and cordage roar and
      whine ;

Loud thunder grumbles ; lightning flashes bright ;
  It rains, it hails, the air becomes opaque—
Wild bolts of fire, flaming clouds their light ;
  One road of foam is seen to be their wake.

Ethereal murmurs join the boiling tides ;
  Air, fire, and sea, rebel in strange contagion.
The ship, as if through ancient chaos, rides,
  With elements in wildest perturbation.

One call'd Panurge then grasp'd the gunwale
    tight,
  Half dead, and, invoking Heaven to his aid,
Declared he would confess and make all right,
  If only once again some land they made.

"Oh! thrice," he cried, "and four times happy
    those
  Who plant their cabbages on any ground ;
For always on it they can one foot pose,
  While still the other near it must be found.

Let men dispute about the Sovereign Good ;
 But cabbage-planting I henceforth declare
Should be by that great term now understood ;
 Of real worth all other states are bare.

Oh, for a lordly manor deific !
 Do give me but a shed of cows or swine !
Ha ! ha ! that wave has made me feel so sick !
 Are we or are we not amidst the brine ?

Give me, O friends, some vinegar, I pray !
 Zalas, the sails are shiver'd to a thread ;
The mainmast now has lost its only stay ;
 Down in the wave it plunges its tall head.

Be be, be be, confiteor—what next ?
 Oh, saintly friar, let me hear thy voice !
Hear—culpa maxima—I'm so perplex'd,
 'Tis now my enemies would all rejoice.

Our ropes are burst ; there is not left a spar.
 To whom, I ask, can we the customs pay ?
Oh, look ! our poor fragments hurl'd, floating far.
 Ye sailors, is it night, or is it day ?

Be, be, be ; bous, bous, bous ! just look you there ;
 The compass, O astrologer, is gone !
I tremble ; wet, dishevell'd is my hair ;
 It all is over, and my course is done.

          L

Bou, bou, bou, bou, bou, bou,—I drown; I
    drown;
  I die, good people all, 'tis more than dread;
O gracious heavens, help! do just look down,
    Or you will find me stark, and blue, and dead."

Now the bold captain meanwhile had implored
    Divine protection with devotion pure;
And after all had pray'd who were on board,
    They flew to take their measures wise and sure.

Thus all, with friar John, would take their place;
    Alone Panurge held fast to weep and cry,
When John, perceiving his dejected face,
    Exclaim'd, " Panurge, O calf, you can but die;

Come and assist, and cease that idle wail."
    " Be, be, be; bous, bous, bous," replied Panurge;
" What could I do, since nothing can avail?
    I cannot bear this raging of the surge.

O John, my father, spiritual friend,
    My uncle and my all, I die, I die—
Amidst these waves I know that I shall end;
    Then suffer me to pray, and weep, and sigh.

Ha! just look there, the water in my shoes!
    Bous, bous, bous; paisch; hu, hu, ha, ha; lo, lo.
See what a course the vessel onward hues!
    I'm the fork'd tree, legs upwards, head below.

Oh that I were now with those honest friars
  Whom we beheld this morning on our road!
Oh, yes! that now would crown all my desires,
  Could I but reach their pure, sweet, blest abode.

Hollo! hollo! hollo! now there's a wave!
  Oh! mea culpa, for we all must sink;
From cruel death there's nothing me can save—
  The sea my bed, the sea my only drink.

Confession! See me on my knees, blest man;
  Your benediction holy grant to me!"
"O slave!" said John, "you will not when
    you can.
  To hear you now the time will not agree;

By thirty legions of the devil's train
  Now rise and help us! Comes he? comes he
    not?"
"Oh, swear not," cried Panurge, "from oaths ab-
    stain,
  To-morrow swear like any drunken sot,

But, oh! not now, my Father and my friend;
  Hollo! hollo! alas! the water gains;
Be, be, be, be—I now draw near my end;
  See! every plank that holds our vessel strains.

L 2

Oh! eighteen hundred thousand crowns for him
  Who helps me to escape to any shore,
Wet though I be, and in such piteous trim
  As never wretched mortal was before.

Confession—zalas, what about my will?"
  "A thousand devils," John cries, "on thy
    head!
Is this a time to write your codicil,
  When you should help us, as I loudly said?

For now or never, would you fly from death,
  It you behoves, like one of us, to toil;"
Panurge replies, "Oh, keep such angry breath,
  My gentle mignon! oh, this dreadful coil!

Bou, bou, bou, bou; and are we doom'd to die?
  To perish drowning, must this be my lot?
Will Heaven not hear my shriek, my piercing
    cry?
  Must all my pleasant drinkings be forgot?"

"Ten million devils," John cries, "bind that
    fast;"
"Oh, swear not," Panurge says, "do not blaspheme.
  Again that wave! I see the die is cast,
And nought from hideous death can me redeem. .

I pardon all the world ; yes, now this once ;
 I die, my friend, adieu ; so farewell now,
Be no more said excepting for the nonce
 I make this steady, constant, faithful vow—

Bous, bous, bous, bous, if e'er I reach the land,
 And out of danger on some friendly shore,
A fine, great, little church I'll build, to stand
 Where sheep, or cows, or goats shall graze no
  more. .

Bous, bous, bous, bous, bous, bous, I cannot see !
 I cannot speak, or edify you more !
I'm filled with water—bee, bee, bee, bee, bee—
 No bottle fuller in a cellar's store.

That instant, while I oped my mouth so wide
 To pray to promise with a saintly vow,
In rush'd between my teeth the swelling tide ;
 Just look, I'm drench'd. In what state am I
  now ?

Yes ; there has enter'd my imploring mouth
 Some eighteen pailfuls of the horrid brine,
All rushing headlong from the north and south.
 How bitter salt, O gentle Father mine !"

" Ah ! sea-calf, down, and under ocean sink,"
   Said John.   " My lads, the devils seem un-
      chain'd,
Or Proserpine accouches now I think ;"
   " To bells they dance, which makes us thus
      be pain'd,"

Cried Panurge.   " Ha ! you sin, my former
   friend,—
   Former I say, for now I nothing am ;
And you are nothing—we have touch'd our end.
   Perhaps I should have let you swear and damn.

Some comfort 'tis to utter senseless cries ;
   As when one, splitting timber with an axe,
Himself to ease, vociferation tries,
   At each blow crying han ! while still he hacks.

Or when at nine-pins we have push'd the ball,
   And some bystander will incline his head,
As if its movement he could thus recall
   From slight divergence whither it was sped.

But all the same—you sin, I say, you sin."
   " He dotes," said John ; " Now, boy, let that
      rope slack.
Quick ; well done, lads, to heroes you're akin."
   But Panurge, wailing, only cried " Alack !"

" Nor sky nor land can any one behold.
 Of the four elements but two are left—
Fire and water. Oh, that it might be told
 When sinking thus, and of all hope bereft,

I found myself at Chinon with the cook,
 There somehow thrown on shore, I know not
  how,
Though to make patties he myself just took ;
 Yes, that would be a wondrous comfort now."

Cried John, " Let drop your anchors ; aft, be-
  ware ;
 That spar is falling ; zounds ! make all there
  tight.
Haul, haul away ! now be collected there,
 Though all the devils ride the blast to-night."

Then Panurge, spying near a sailor old,
 Just raised his head, and feebly, faintly spoke,
Like some poor wretch, half frozen with the cold,
 Whose chattering teeth seem pity to invoke.

" Good shipman," whispering, " cast me now
  ashore ;
 They say you can such wondrous things
  achieve ;
My pots and saucepans, yes, and all my store
 I'll give you, and indeed I'll not deceive.

Consider how my life is precious, dear ;
    'Tis not a case like some who wish to die ;
Oh ! if at Chinon you were ever near,
    You'd know the fact, and never me deny.

Where are we ? in what depth ! Oh, cast the lead ;"
    From Scylla to Charybdis now we pass ;
Oh, make some vow,"—"to devils, then," John
    said.
    Replies Panurge, " John damns himself alas !

Oh, what a friend I lose in losing him !
    But say some word about my will I must,
Before I float away to sink, not swim ;
    For to a testament I always trust."

" Of what avail," said John, " you frighten'd fool ?
    For either we escape or we are lost.
If we escape, 'twill be a useless tool ;
    And if we die, to whom will it be toss'd ?"

" To some one walking on the beach," he said ;
    " As when Ulysses on the shore was thrown,—
And then for me, thus in a shipwreck dead,
    Some stately cenotaph my name will own,

Raised by some princess pitying my fate,
    Like that Æneas built on Trojan shore
To Deiphobus, as old poets state,
    Or like some hundreds in the times before."

" You dream!" cried John, " I am half madden'd
    made ;
Now, by five hundred million cartloads full
Of devils, come and join with us to aid ;
    Come, lend a hand. Just take this rope and
    pull.

What! our brave captain, you too at your prayers !
    Will no one hope but I unto the last ?
See now how wildly at me each one stares,
    As if all means of safety now were past."

" Alas !" cried Panurge, " be, be, be, be, bou.
    Will nothing melt the heavens to interfere,
To send me some good dolphin ? Oh, pray do !
    And I Arion mount and nothing fear.

Come, gentle dolphin, lead me to the land,
    And all will praise thy timely, gracious care.
I'll play the harp so sweetly at command,
    That thou wilt wish thou could'st be always
    there."

" Land ! land !" they cry, " behold ! it stretches
    clear ;
Unwrapp'd at once the sea, and shore, and sky ;
O'er the red waves of sunset it seems near.
    A harbour's mouth itself we can descry ;

The liquid mountains urge us toward the shore.
  Their sweep, you'd think, must needs us over-
      whelm;
Let us but steer her, danger is no more;
  Let all hands help to bind and keep the helm.

She mounts aloft, and now the breakers roar.
  That wave you'd think would all her planks
      divide.
Hold hard, and only keep her off the shore;
  And let her enter with the rushing tide.

There! now she plunges to rise higher still;
  Another mountain lifts us to the pier.
Will she bear up to pass it? Yes, she will!
  Lift up your hearts, my lads, no more of fear."

"Be, be, be, be; bous, bous," cried Panurge, "still
  We are not yet beyond the force of waves!"
" No," said the pilot, " but you shortly will.
  Praised be our God, who thus delivers, saves!"

" Saint John," cried Panurge, " now indeed you
      speak.
  Oh, the sweet words! that's something like a
      tongue;
But still I feel my limbs and all are weak."
  While, doubtful still, his hands he only wrung.

Then the brave captain cries, "Our aim we win;
  And see what crowds of people line the shore.
The bar once pass'd, the tide must take us in.
  But who's that stretch'd, whom I mark'd not
    before,

Who groans so loud, and looks distracted, wild?"
  "It is," said John, "Panurge, that frighten'd
    wretch,
Who all the time has wept like any child;
  And who could only grasp, and gasp, and
    stretch."

"Well," said the captain, "there was cause to
    fear.
  If fear a valiant man can ever suit,
I do not say it is when death is near,
  As if with holy men I would dispute;

Death in itself presenting nought to dread;
  But it is death at sea that needs must scare;
For when we sink o'erwhelm'd in ocean's bed,
  Who is there left for us to say a prayer?"

To perish in the sea, old Homer said,
  Was thing abhorrent from which nature flew;
And so Æneas wish'd he had been dead,
  By Diomedes slain with all his crew,

Before the tempest on Sicilian shore
  Assail'd his vessels; and he would have died,
Yea, thrice and four times happy long before,
  Amidst the flames that quench'd the Trojan
    pride.

But lo! our ship approaches to the quay;
  And truly still we're in a precious plight.
Let us to shore, and find some speedy way
  To make repairs and set all things to right."

"Ha! ha!" cried Panurge, "all goes well at last.
  But stop, I pray you, let me go the first;
I have some business now the storm is past;
  For things about me are all split and burst;

Or do you want my help, say, longer here?
  That rope do you desire I should coil?
You know my courage notwithstanding fear;
  And how for you I am prepared to toil.

A little fear I had; but what of that?
  The tenth wave raging like an avalanche;
Devoted, ready there I ever sat,
  With real valour ever true and staunch.

Now haul," he cries, "that rope, you there aloft.
  What! you do nothing, idle brother John?
Is this a time to drink, companion soft?
  Ah! what then will you when ashore I'm gone?

How know we but a storm may still succeed?
    Must I again to your assistance fly?
Oh! truly I repent me, yes, indeed,
    That those wise sages I did once decry,

Who said to take a walk along the sea,
    And practise navigation near the land,
Safe and delectable must always be;
    A doctrine which, though late, I understand.

As if you held your horse tight by the bridle,
    Walking securely on your feet the while.
Ah! that's the pastime for a man not idle,
    Who would still cheat misfortune and beguile.

Ha! ha! By heavens all goes now right well.
    To lend a hand do you invite me yet?
The devil take me if I let you tell
    That you on sea or land I could forget."

Now an old sailor, who had heard them all,
    To the brave captain said, "My chief, look
       here—
The wounds I had obeying still your call,
    Though quite as much as Panurge feeling fear.

But then I thought that I must help you still;
    And if it happen'd that there die I must,
I should be but fulfilling Heaven's high will,
    In which alone I needs must ever trust.

No danger present—then's the time to cry;
    But while it lasts, 'tis deeds, not words, we
        want;
This is the true devotion—honour high;
    When safe I'd pray and scorn every taunt;

Yes, then I'd pray to God just like the rest;
    But when occasion needs that we should toil,
If I don't labour, well indeed I'm blest;
    Since praying then would be but mere turmoil.

And if to watch and work I then resort,
    While only hypocrites implore and weep,
I shall most likely gain the happy port,
    When their sham vows in vain will safety seek."

" Let me consort with devils," cried out John,
    (" I'm half with you and them," then Panurge
        said)
" If you have not the first right to be gone
    To feast and sing, and some loved beauty wed."

Then " Vogue la galère !" Panurge sung aloud;
    " This brother John does nought but sermonize.
Come, help, you idle knave, and bind that shroud;
    You're good for nothing with your airs so wise.

Still looking vainly on at me who work
 To aid this brave man, whom I like to find
Not such as you, a lazy, dreaming Turk,
 But one who has with me accordant mind."

" Now three words more; my friend, just answer
  me.
 What thickness have ships' sides? pray, are
  they thin?"
" Two good wide inches guard you from the sea;"
 " Of death two fingers then we are within!

Is this of marriage one of the nine joys?"
 " He measures," said the sailor, " peril now
But with the yard of fear that he employs."
 " I have no fear," cries Panurge, " that I vow;

My name is William, who fear never felt;
 With courage, I mean not like that of sheep,
But wolfine courage that will never melt,
 Or murderer's, that kills men when asleep.

I fear but danger; now you know my will.
 Yon boy, approach; I'll land me from your
  boat.
God speed you all, or do you need me still?
 I feel a thirst to aid you while afloat.

Oh! spare me not, for love of God, I say.
   Adam (that's man) to labour thus was born,
As the wing'd bird pursues his constant way;
   Yes, day and night, at noon, and eve, and morn.

'Tis Heaven's just will that we should earn our
      bread
   By sweat and care; and never, like that friar,
That idle John, so quick to feel a dread,
   Who never can with eating, drinking tire.

Oh! what a beauteous port, and handsome race
   Of people standing ranged along the shore!
Knew I but love, I'd kiss each smiling face.
   What calm! what weather bright Heaven has
      in store!"

"Now by the frock I wear," said brother John,
   "Without all reason was your terror late;
For mark my words, when I am dead and gone,
   To die in water will not be your fate.

Aloft in air methinks I see thee swing.
   Who is there wants a cloak against the rain?
Leave fur of wolves and badgers, all that thing,
   And in the skin of Panurge dry remain.

Not safe from fire; no, that I never said;
  So pass not near where smiths cause sparks to
    fly.
Enflamed you'd see it, or like ashes dead,
  And scorch'd in it you then yourself might die.

But to the rain expose it when you will,
  To hail or snow,—or when you take a plunge
Beneath the ocean, dry you will be still,
  No wet absorbing like a porous sponge.

Make of it winter-boots, you'll have dry feet,
  Or bladders to teach youths and boys to swim.
They'll quickly learn all for that art meet
  To float securely as you'd have seen him."

"Panurge, my friend, no water ever dread;
  By other element you're doom'd to die.
You're safe o'er lake, o'er ocean, river, sped;
  The case is alter'd when to trees you're nigh."

"Well, be it so," said Panurge; "but the Cooks
  Of devils may mistake, as others do,
To boil what should be roasted with their hooks,
  Their error great, and I have seen it too.

But hear me, friends; the church that I did vow
  Before this noble company of late,
I do not care to found or build it now;
  Or, what I meant by it, just let me state.

M

A church of rose-water I understood,
　In which no cow or sheep should ever graze,
Or I would cast it to the depths for good,
　Where thing aquatic only thrives, and stays."

" Lo ! here's the gallant Christian," they all cried,
　" Who verifies the Lombard proverb old—
' The bridge once pass'd, the saint is soon defied.'
　Draw you the moral, for the tale is told."

The moral—yes, there's much that's plain and
　　　well,
　But more that in the heart should deeply sink.
I heed not who the story first did tell ;
　For it can make us pause, refrain, and think ;

Think like the great and holy at their prayers—
　Think like the sons of honour when they
　　　wrought ;
Imbibing what our nature all repairs—
　A love of truth—the highest flight of thought—

When we would mount to regions of the grand,
And everlastingly unshaken stand.

THE COMIC LOOKING-GLASS[4].

WITHIN the garden's pale, so varied, fair,
  Are plants and shrubs that seem of comic form ;
The cactus strange, and monkey-trees are there,
  Of prickly, bulbous things, an endless swarm.

The medlars, too, used often to be found,
  Which the French call a fruit of fantasy ;
While in some flowers, ranged along the ground,
  A laughing emblem others think they see.

A vicious nature suits not laughter free ;
  But yet an aspect ludicrous it wears,
When, passing near that ill-condition'd tree,
  We mark the hard crabb'd fruit it always bears.

Oh! let no gentle face grow deadly pale
  With deep disgust, of malice when I sing ;
It is in antique French I find the tale,
  Which shows the horror of that odious spring.

[4] Translated from old French.

M 2

Come, young men tall, for you I'll touch the lyre;
Yourselves, I trust, you shortly will admire,
When in this odious glass you find no trace
Of your own inward, constant, harmless face.
Ne'er ruffled by revenge, that lust of brutes,
Which gentle human nature never suits;
Though rage vindictive has been known to rise
From even Love, who should all vice despise.
While laughable indeed is each detail,
Your laughter often is of much avail;
Joy or amendment the result will be,
The theme is therefore all of charity.
It skills not always citing special names,
And least of all when such a usage shames;
But here Panurge and Epistemon both
Must be announced, however we are loth.

Two ships were passing gaily o'er the sea,
The ocean calm as it could ever be;
The one of friends contain'd a merry crew,
The other was by merchants freighted new.
They spoke, they touch'd, and visits interchanged;
The sea so tranquil, nought was disarranged.
It chanced that Panurge (jolly dog was he)
Should with a merchant come to disagree.
High words were pass'd, they even threaten'd
    blows;
I skip o'er vile scenes the world elsewhere shows.
The quarrel over, with the help of friends,
Each then some glasses on the other spends;

All thought the reconciliation true,
But what would follow there was no one knew.

Panurge then said in Epistemon's ear—
" Do you and all withdraw and make good cheer ;
I'll have some fun, that merchant silly make ;
The show succeeds if not a cord I break."
So with the merchant drinking once again,
He soon proposed to do some business plain,
Just begging him to sell one of his sheep,
Saying that thereby he would profit reap.
" Alas! my friend, our neighbour," he replied,
" How skill'd you are poor people to deride !
Methinks much rather would you cut a purse
Than practise buying sheep to tend and nurse."
" To triumph that way, sooth, you have the air,
But keeping sheep is mine, not your affair."
Said Panurge, " Leaving special grace, just say,
" You'll sell one sheep and let me have my way.
How much ?" The merchant look'd him in the
            face.
" You seem, my friend, their value not to trace.
Observe these fleeces ; Jason took of old
From one of them the far-famed fleece of gold.
The House of Burgundy its order drew
From these,—now worn by chevaliers preux.
They come from Eastern shores, of lineage high."
" Agreed," said Panurge, " one of them I'd buy.

How much ?" " My friend," the merchant gravely
        said,
" Hear in your other ear ; just turn your head."
" At your desire."   " Outward bound ?"   " Yes :
    why ?"
" To see the world gaily ?   Don't deny.
Behold that sheep, and mark his plaintive voice ;
To hear him *bah* does all my heart rejoice.
Now let a pact be struck between us both ;
To enter one scale be you nothing loth,
While in the other let that sheep be found ;
Then hoist the balance, and I will be bound
To pay a hundred oysters from the rocks
If he sinks not and all your boasting mocks ;
While you will dance and dangle in the air,
Your future end, as now predict I dare."

" Patience," said Panurge secretly, " but still,
Do sell me one, and let me have my will."
" My friend," replied the merchant, " neighbour
        sweet,
I love with open honesty to treat.
From fleeces such is cloth of Rouen made,
Which casts all other clothing in the shade.
The skin yields leather to Montelimar,
Best Russian, Spanish—all surpassing far.
The gut, for violins' and banjoes' strings,
In price surpasses all that Munich brings.

What think you?" "May it please you," Panurge
     said,
"Now sell me one. How much? and nothing
     dread."
Then pulling out his purse he show'd the gold.
"Come, strike a bargain, and the sheep is sold."
"My friend," replied the merchant, "neighbour
     mine,
I see the glitter; gold will always shine.
But this is meat for princes and for kings,
The flesh more delicate than sweetest things.
On you I never worthless stuff would palm;
Of these the odour and the taste are balm.
I bring them from a country where the pigs
(Now Heaven be with us) eat no food but figs;
The sows (save all respect for those around)
On orange-flowers feed that spread the ground."
"Well, sell me one," said Panurge, "I will pay
Like any king, the price you only say.
Courage, merchant! How much? Lay it on;
I will not haggle, '*foy de pieton.*'"
"My friend," replied the merchant, "neighbour
     dear,
This race across the Hellespont, I hear,
Did carry Phrixus, as the tale is told;
Such sires had all these in the times of old.
Excretæ, theirs, you understand me well,
For sums enormous you can always sell.
These, in fact, prove the best of all manure;
They (save your reverence) diseases cure.

For seventy-eight descriptions in our land
'Tis the specific doctors all command.
What think you, friend and neighbour?"   "Well,
    I say,
Name but your price, and I will quickly pay."
"My friend," the merchant said, "my neighbour
    prized,
Can you see nature's wonders not surprised?
Reflect a little on these marvels all,
Made to astonish, charm, and appal.
Just take these horns, useless as you see,
With knife or hatchet split (all one to me),
Then plant their points, oft water'd, in the
    ground ;
The best asparagus will there be found,—
And not excepting, as you might suppose,
That kind so famed which at Ravenna grows.
I know not," adds the merchant, " if you be
A clerk to ponder deep divinity ;
But now show me horns such as these, and I
Will wonder much, and nothing you deny.
I know not if you be a married man ;
But try now to match these horns if you can."
Still patience ! secretly then Panurge thought ;
The merchant yet would speak, fresh reasons
    brought.
" Then apropos of clerks, you would have known,
These sheep's feet have below a little bone
With which of old men fabricated dice,
At which Augustus lost once in a trice

Still more than fifty thousand crowns in play;
Now to these marvels what have you to say?
So when you have consider'd all the parts—
The shoulders, legs, loins, breasts, the kidneys,
      hearts,
The bladder for the ball that highest bounds—
The heads, to yield decoctions for your hounds "—
The captain, growing angry, cried "Enough!"
His look, his tone, his gestures, all were rough.
"Enough, enough! Will you despatch anon?
Sell or refuse, and let the man begone."
If you now wish to sell, run on no more
With all that slang in such confounded store."
"I ask no better," said the merchant gay;
"For love of you I'll sell it if I may;
But, choosing, he must pay two livres down "
"Tournoys," Panurge replied, "why in our town
I could have five or six for such a price;
Reflect again; abatement in a trice.
You're not the first who, wishing to be rich,
Too quickly found, and to his cost, a hitch."
"A quartain fever seize you, heavy fool,"
Replied the merchant; "you're uncommon cool.
The least of these is worth some four times
      more
Than sheep you purchase on the Spanish shore,
And pay for each a talent all of gold."
Said Panurge, "Blessed Sir, how you can scold!
Methinks that in harness you too warm grow;
But take your money quickly, even so;"

Then lifting up the sheep, which bleated loud,
The others follow'd, bleating in a crowd.
"Oh! don't he choose the best?" the merchant
        cried.
The rascal knew it, while he me defied.
The Lord of Candale would have prized it well ;
'Tis he who can a good from bad one tell.

Then suddenly, I know not how to say,
All pass'd so quickly that I never may.
No time I had to mark, distinguish aught ;
The whole was done before I could have thought.
Panurge, in silence, overboard did throw
That bleating sheep, which bleated still below ;
The rest, all bleating, jump'd into the sea ;
Each only sought that he might quickest be
To follow that companion from the file—
Impossible to hold them back the while ;
For such is nature in that sottish beast,
The first all follow, greatest and the least.
The merchant, in an agony of fear,
Took hold of each as each would pass him near.
With force he clutched a fat and sturdy sheep,
And hoped by holding him the rest to keep.
But such was that sheep's wondrous mighty
        strength,
He pull'd the merchant after him at length.
Remaining shepherds did the same for others,
Until the sea both sheep and shepherds smothers ;

They held on by the horns, the fleece, or feet—
A watery death they all alike did meet.
Panurge look'd on, and, armèd with a spar,
Kept all the strugglers from the vessel far,
Preventing them from clinging to a plank,
Until, exhausted, they fell back and sank ;
And then, triumphant, cried out as he stood,
"Never a mortal man has done me good
Without some recompense or thanks at least.
With gracious words I own I often ceased.
Never a man has injured me, and I
To pay him off could find no remedy.
I am not stupid quite to that degree,
So now you understand the sum of me."

Well, then, before you is my mirror hung,
Of which, I believe, no poet ever sung.
Can any hearer find in it a trace
Of his own secret undiscover'd face ?
May his remorse, then, justify my pains,
And yield a dignity to comic strains.
Oh ! henceforth may he that whole type deride,
That so may end all worldly selfish pride ;
To put on charity, that sweetest stole,
And so forget and renovate the whole.

THE SEIGNEUR DE BASCHÉ.

WHILE breathing now this balmy air perfumed
    from all the flowers,
How can we think beside us here that Litigation
    lours?
But if sweet children here will play, and dance,
    and sing, still Law
Will have his Courts and temples too, from which
    some mischief draw.
Methinks these poplars, aspens pale, have learnt
    thus all to quiver,
From hearing tales of clients sad, which caused
    them white to shiver.
Leaves that the slightest breath of wind can force
    to tremble so
May be excused for dancing thus to songs of legal
    woe.
But now it is not I would sing, the theme to me is
    bad;
So list to what my Bard relates, and mirth can
    yet be had.
In prose he tells it, what of that? for doggrel
    childhood wins.
His fun to rhyme will come so pat; but hush! he
    now begins.

I'll sing a ship that sail'd along by Procuration
    Isle,
The place all strange, but there we said we ought
    to stop a while.
The country was all blotted, scratch'd, and with
    erasures stain'd ;
Of that we could make nothing, sooth, the time
    that we remain'd.
For there did reign chicanery of every colour and
    hair ;
To eat or drink there was no man who did invite
    us there.
Only with great reverences, prolong'd and multi-
    plied,
They offer'd all their services, and said they'd take
    our side
For payment, understand that well,—I would not
    you mislead ;
And then we heard, described at length, the life
    they all did lead.
Their ways in fact were quite opposed to those
    all elsewhere known ;
As when you hear me, I conceive, that you must
    quickly own.
For elsewhere men are boist'rous, rough ; they
    kick, and beat, and kill ;
But here they live by being beat'n, and so fulfil
    their will.
And if for any length of time they get no beating
    sound,

They die of hunger—children, wife, while all
    complain around.
When lawyers, usurers, owe spite to any gentle-
    man,
They send their agents, some of these, to plague
    him all they can.
They cite, adjourn, then outrage him, and with
    such impudence,
That he must hit them right and left, unless de-
    prived of sense.
Unless quite paralytic grown, he patient must
    abide
The taunts of insolence, and worse, of avarice and
    pride ;
To sink into this abject state he must be then
    resign'd,
Deprived of all the noble fire he thought he had
    in mind ;
Or send them flying o'er the wall of his bold castle
    fair ;
And then they triumph and rejoice, for all their
    gain lies there.
They then are rich for many months, they seek
    for reparation,
The gentleman may lose his all to feed that
    hungry nation.
The Lord of Basché, nathless found a way to
    cure them all ;
"Just listen, now," the pilot said, " to what did
    them befall.

One day as he was just return'd from many a
    noble fight,
Appear'd one of these chicaners who him did duly
    cite.
Then sad he grew, as well he might, but being
    free and gay,
He ask'd his curate, baker too, to dine with him
    that day.
To them he said abruptly thus, his servants all
    around,
'See, my dear children, how these knaves will
    grind me to the ground.
If you don't try to help me now, I think, and say,
    and swear,
That straight to Turks and all the devils I will
    soon repair.
So when these lawyers come again, you, baker,
    with your wife,
With you, my curate, and the rest, make ready for
    the strife.
Your wife I'll call my 'fianced bride; the curate
    in his stole
Will seem to join our hands together; the castle
    bells may toll.
The bride once kiss'd, you know the custom of
    this fair countree,
You hit all present with your fists to keep up
    memory.
But for the lawyer, let him feel your blows in
    earnest, strong;

So hit, and daub, and maul him well; no violence
    is wrong.
And he who best can draw his blood my friend
    shall ever be
Esteem'd the first; you have your cue, and do all
    cheerfully.
Fear no citation for the deed; bosh! custom
    covers all.
So only be attentive then to hear the first loud
    call.
With play and laughter do you all; go to, and
    nothing dread;
You'll sup the better, and for the rest I'll answer
    with my head.
"But how shall I the lawyer know?" the porter
    then exclaim'd,
"So many strangers pass the gate, their calling
    never named?"
Said Basché, "When you see arrive a man in
    black, and thin,
Wearing a clumsy silver ring, who asks to pass
    within,
Still grasping tight a faded bag, and, smiling,
    cringing low,
Be courteous, and permission free be sure you
    then bestow.
But quickly sound your bell, and we will hasten
    for the nonce.
The tragic comedy begins with vengeance all at
    once."

It chanced that very day should come a citer old
    and red,
And on his left thumb was a ring exactly as was
    said ;
He carried on an ugly mule a bag that seem'd to
    burst ;
'Twas fill'd with informations, all just as was said
    at first.
The porter bow'd right graciously, and bade him
    hasten on,
For fear the marriage-guests so gay should all
    have fed and gone.
"You come," he said, "in joyous hour, by plates
    and dishes all
The whole now passes merrily within my master's
    hall.
Yet stop to drink a moment here, there still is
    ever time.
Hark! hark! the tabors and the pipes, with all
    the pleasant chime."
While the grim Lawyer drank his cups, the Curate
    and the rest
Donn'd all their robes, and each prepared, be sure,
    to do his best.
The Lawyer then proceeded, grave, with many
    bows and scrapes,
To reach the hall, when from his bag a parch-
    ment grim he takes,—
Entreated Basché to excuse his task unpleasant
    there,

N

Alleging that a public man must all things
    grievous dare,
Declaring he would do the same for him when he
    should call—
Yes, yes, and for the smallest Page within that
    castle hall.
" No more, no more," replied the Lord ; " you do
    your duty, man.
But first and foremost you must drink ; be hearty,
    if you can.
For this is now my wedding-day, so let no man be
    grave ;
I think you'll soon behold a set that will both
    dance and rave."
The Curate mumbled then some words ; the Lord
    he kiss'd his bride ;
You need not ask if blows began, like rain, on
    every side.
" 'Tis wedding, wedding-feast," they cry, " be
    sure you don't forget ;
Take that, and that, you silly Page, you're not
    half pommell'd yet.
But when to chicaner it came at last to be his
    turn,
Ha ! ha ! each struck in earnest then, as each warm
    heart did burn.
The upper-lip, dismantled, soon did hang upon his
    chin,
With denudation absolute of all that lay with-
    in.

The molar, masticating teeth, canine, the wise and
   all—
While fast as hailstones on his back the youthful
   fists did fall.
One eye was poach'd in butter black; eight ribs
   were snapp'd away;
The lower jaw was fricasee'd; but all was done in
   play.
"Oh! call you that the play of youth?" the
   lawyer loudly cried;
"That this is play, before the court shall stoutly
   be denied."
But still they laugh'd, with laughter wept; the
   tears ran from each eye;
Their sides they scarce with laughing hold, while
   still their blows they ply.
Then breach of continuity appear'd in all his
   skin;
While all his bones were bruised, and bent, and
   shatter'd worse within.
"Good Lord!" he cried, "now shiver'd, smither'd,
   riddled in my heel!
While pounded, rounded, and confounded all myself I feel."
But "Custom, custom," still they cried, "'tis wedding custom now;
Such play and romps all must expect, though lawyers shout and vow."
But what could men of law object? he fared with
   others there;

Only unto a wedding-feast he would no more
    repair.

Return'd home, he Basché praised for giving him
    such wine;

For all went well right merrily, and all he said
    did shine,

Until the vulgar youth began to strike; 'twas
    quite their fault;

But all the same, for future feasts let other guests
    be sought.

By help of surgeons then he lived as long as you
    desire;

But, sooth, to mention him again no one would
    others tire.

His memory was past and gone when bells had
    ceased to sound

For his interment, when he lay forgotten in the
    ground.

From that time forth the country knew that
    Basché's gold was not

For chicaners or lawyers sly, that plaguing, nasty
    lot.

Lord Basché ever afterwards had peace and sweet
    repose.

Of "Basché's wedding," proverb grown, that
    whole wide country knows.

Now hoist your sails, ye gallant tars, and let us
    hence be sped;

That island with its inky shores afflicts our soul
    with dread.

Besides, a progress here is made, and these are
    wiser grown ;
There's no escaping now their snares ; such cus-
    toms they disown.
The bows and cringes may remain, the payment
    too as well,
But once within their clutches strong, a sadder
    tale you'd tell.
Then spread the main sheet to the wind, and seek
    another shore,
Where lawyers and chicanery are never heard of
    more.

TO PART.

Oh ! look how the green leaf falls !
    Though cluster'd with others it grew,
Skimming o'er fences and walls,
    How far before sinking it flew.

Dews of the morning it drank ;
    The sun threw gold light all around ;
And yet on the grass it sank,
    While not the least warning was found.

Faint winds pass sighing along ;
    One by one then its fellows drop,
As, moved by their gentle song,
    No longer united to stop.

These leaves, all emblems of men,
  Will part and abandon their spray,
Further to fly off, and then—
  To flutter and so pass away.

Not only leaves, but their race
  Will migrate to far distant lands,
Some whom the tempest will chase,
  While obeying its stern commands.

Then some by autumnal wind
  Are carried aloft to the sea,
Where floating, mariners find
  How wafted far off they can be.

Jericho's rose from the sand
  Of Egypt and Syria has fled,
Thus at the breeze's command,
  To decorate Europe's fair head.

Rivers and brooks others choose
To pass on their fugitive wave,
  Their own dear country to lose
While novelties seeking to brave.

" If I were the leaf," you cry [5],
  " That so turns at every wind,
Detach'd from my branch I'd fly,
  And me nothing local should bind.

[5] Victor Hugo.

I'd fling myself to the breeze
  Which in the bright morning would blow;
I'd gladly forsake the trees
  For the stream from the West below.

Beyond the river that glides,
  Beyond the dark forests so vast,
Beyond vales where gloom abides,
  I'd have fled far, and ran, and pass'd

Beyond all the plains so bare,
  Beyond all the oaks and the lime,
Beyond wild animals' lair,
  Beyond where the chamois will climb.

And where, poor fugitive, now,
  Would you stop, and at last remain,
When you grew once from your bough
  Without any cause to complain?

At length you would seek to rest
  Where what is now present can be,
In the heart of some one blest,
  Just like her who now smiles on thee.

Then wherefore anxious to fly,
  Like leaves that are senseless and cold,
When here by your side can lie
  The whole sum of all you'd behold?

Oh, why, O my heart, oh, why
    Must we, whose existence is love,
Thus worship a tearful sigh,
    And from half of ourselves remove?

Have we not sunshine and flowers,
    With the perfume of air around?
Why, then, forsake our fond bowers,
    Where the friend of our heart is found?

What can be sweeter than love
    Return'd, or even but given?
Oh! why, then, should one remove,
    Just as if by some demon driven?

Must such be our restless will,
With present things never at ease,
    That nothing quiet and still
Can for any time wholly please?

Ants that have traversed the sky
    But once, when returned to home,
Resolve never more to fly,
    No longer so wanton to roam.

With joy they part with their wings,
    By themselves or by others torn,
Their nest then such pure joy brings;
    While wandering saw them forlorn.

The poor silent plant can feel;
    Sensibility marks that reign;
It shrinks when breezes reveal
    That a time approaches of pain.

We know too all that's in store,
    Even far when we wish to fly;
Perhaps we shall see no more
    The lov'd friend for whom we would die.

And yet, and yet we rush on,
    Thus recklessly meeting our fate;
Impatient till we are gone,
    As if flying to what we hate.

Is it to-morrow we part?
    Ah! how quickly that word is said!
And feel we no poignant dart
    To think that now one must be fled?

'Tis a knell so solemn—" *Part*,"
    And observe how it mocks our rhyme,
First always suggesting " *heart*,"
    As if with deep funeral chime.

Oh! why must that word affect
    Ev'ry tongue that is known to man?
As if it announced defect
    In God's gracious and wondrous plan?

Though all Nature's laws still seek
  A union which nothing divides;
And yet here they seem so weak
  That them all our feeling derides.

What's "*Part*" when we meet so soon?
  But the future still no one knows.
Tush! Each fresh meeting's a boon!
  Ay, but Time still the living mows.

Disguise it then as you will;
  "*To part*" is a tragical sound!
We needs must feel lone and chill
  As it tolls thus and floats around!

But Faith will then sound to aid,
  Louder telling that union here
Proves but a flickering shade,
  Whatever may shine or appear.

'Tis elsewhere that union reigns,
  Where our language and all are new,
"*Part*" a word foreign in strains
  Where our friends are ever in view.

ON THE MARRIAGE OF THE HON. P. S.

WHILE bright leaves are dancing above and
    around,
A sweet merry theme now for me has been found.
Pray, what does Creation proclaim from its birth,
But union, and marriage, and wisdom, and mirth
The woodbine, whose perfume we all of us know,
In autumn has berries it proudly may show;
It borrows some strength from a branch that is
    nigh;   [vie.
With the grace that it lends there's nothing can
That branch it invests with a beauteous festoon,
While unconscious itself of its own bright boon,
In twining so closely to some hard rough tree,
Like the love of a woman mysteriously.
For mark that it is to the right they will twine,
Like convolvulus white, or the fair woodbine.
But leaving these emblems for one I will sing
Expanding a tiny, but true, fervent wing.

Oh! wonder not, Pauline, if, absent, I stray,
    While songs hymeneal will float o'er thy
        bower;
True joy would I know well thence drive me
    away,   [hour.
    Howe'er I may pass, while unseen, that bright

The heart that distrusts still its own gayest
    beams
  Would shrink from a lustre that owns no alloy,
Not daring to blend with it only what seems
  Where still it can no unmix'd radiance employ.

The bark that now enters so gaily the port
  Would see with regret a lone wreck near the
    shore,
Where only some harpies and wild birds resort,
  And innocent pleasure can frolic no more.

The train that triumphantly swept o'er the rail,
  Which some strange destruction a ruin has left,
Is always removed as of no more avail,
  Of all future promise so wholly bereft.

Dost mark with what speed all its fragments are
    swept
  Away from the sight of the next who pass
    near?
Enough! let catastrophes elsewhere be wept;
  But traces like these must for them disappear.

Then blame not survivors if now all bereft,
  They wish not a gloomy memento to shine;
Unheard let them keep to themselves what is left,
  With pleasures distemper'd, perhaps, just like
    mine.

You still have their wishes, deep breathed from
    the heart,
  That Eden's true joys ever round thee may be,
Though idly they waste their affectionate dart;
  Without such they wait upon each that's like
    thee.

But let me not ask you e'en pity to blend
  With all the pure raptures prepared for you
    there;
For Circumstance still can accomplish some end,
  To hope or conceive which our thoughts will
    not dare.

Time, Chance, and Occasion, blind chance as we
    say,
  Most mortals on earth will still potently move;
While poets think all things are sport to their
    sway,
  Yes, all things but souls led by Infinite Love.

Grim Circumstance! yes, let all mercy invoke!
  Let Circumstance rule still, exhausting its store
On those whom it ceased not with nets to provoke
  Till, caught and entangled, they gasp'd on the
    shore.

'Tis Mercy that can and may all reunite ;
 Then let no cloud pass o'er this sweet happy
   day ;
For all can have hopes and blest visions most
  bright
 Of joy when for ever our fears pass away.

THE LONELY BENCH.

LET drooping willows weep their fill,
Their pensive branches sweep the rill ;
  There is a woe
No tree can typify to thought,
Though all thy mind to that be brought,
  And pensive grow.

A thing most delicate indeed,
Congenial with the lover's creed,
  Is desolation.
On earth it walks not, poets say ;
It floats not on aerial way ;
  It has its station

In the large tender heart, and best
Where its soft silent footsteps rest
  On Hope that's fled.
There it still fans, with faint, pale wing,
Remembrance, till it needs must sing
  Of what is dead.

The birch, that "Lady of the Wood"
On barren rocks has often stood ;
    But who will see
The graceful, airy Being fond,
All hope of being found beyond,
    Again with thee ?

One lonely leaf upon a bough
In winter, no companions now,
    Might yet pourtray
The fleeting, pale, and blighted state
Of one so wholly desolate,
    Who thus must stray.

That season would with all combine ;
When no ray in the heart would shine,
    'Tis clouds and cold ;
The leaves, from branches torn, pass ;
All nature seems to cry Alas !
    Behold ! behold !

You stray alone, no spirits left,
In solitude of all bereft,
    Hope even fled ;
What friend would gladly join you here ?
What sprite would not such silence fear,
    Where joys are dead ?

But why will not come others known,
To sit and think with you alone,
    With you to stray?
Is it in you that all decays,
And youth will dread such pensive ways,
    To thoughts a prey?

What! dead! already in the ground!
Such Beings without looks or sound!
    Such flowers past!
Oh! let me tread the wither'd leaves;
Their gloom at least no heart deceives,
    Around it cast.

The dance! she loved it all too well.
The dance! it proved for her a spell;
    I gather all *
From one who paints a sister flower,
Once that grew up within his bower,
    Who loved the ball.

Three days and nights she would before,
Upon the fête so ponder, pore,
    That in her sleep
The lights, the music, and the glee,
All join'd in one vast harmony,
    Round her to keep.

* Partly from the French.

And then, when dress'd with all things right,
She hastens, wild with joy, and bright,
    To hear the strain—
To join the throng, to aid the dance,
To feel her life a blissful trance!
    But who again

Will see that step, that smile, that air,
So light, so innocent, so fair,
    That childish joy,
As in a dream that paints a fairy
All grace and beauty, spirit, airy—
    A living toy,

That sparkled like a diamond bright,
That dazzled all who came in sight
    Of such a grace?
Ah! where is that companion now?
Oh! let me haunt the broken bough,
    In dark woods pace.

Farewell the dance and laugh so loud
That child-like rang amidst the crowd;
    Farewell the friend
Who here with me would sit to tell
How all did pass so wondrous well,
    And find no end.

Now, midst the leaves when falling all,
You watch and see her in the ball,
　　Where *they* must dance,
Fast whirling in the sombre shade,
So pale, like them, a spectre made,
　　A dream, a trance!

But oh! how quickly now has fled
She who at last would deck her head
　　With pensive flowers!
Like poor Ophelia in the brook,
Raising at length a longing look
　　Towards Heaven's own bowers!

Such visions pass, and soon are gone,
And men are left to think alone—
　　Yes, just like thee—
While other friends that yet remain
Are not so quickly found again
　　With them to be.

No longer now for them the dawn,
The bliss from setting radiance drawn,
　　So Hugo sings.
Their hearts, as if with cold fogs fed,
Resemble earth when leaves are dead,
　　No more with wings.

If morn or eve they find the grass
Quite wet beneath the feet that pass,
    They only say,
It is the rain, and not the dew,
As when a happy time we knew,
    Now fled away.

Such pauses sometimes in our life
Exceed in bitterness its strife,
    Its sternest blows;
That sense of being left to think,
As if deserted on a brink,
    Is more than woes.

It has no voice; it has no claim;
It has no ground; it has no name;
    It lies too deep;
It preys, unseen, upon the heart,
Upon each warm and vital part;
    It cannot weep;

It only calls back what is past—
What did but some few short years last;
    Bids you compare
The friendly chat, the loving eyes,
The rapture which did both surprise—
    With present care!

No social link to join your mind
With those you love of human kind—
   All isolation !
Like a lone ice-bound vessel, far
Around you one vast snowy bar—
   Blank desolation !

A stranded wreck deserted there ;
From far the circling sun so fair
   Will tell of lands
With summer beams embathed in light ;
But they are hidden from your sight,
   Midst frozen strands,

Where only phantoms prowl and moan,
Concordant with the strange wild tone
   Of Nature round ;
While plains where ice alone is green,
And gulfs, unfathom'd, yawn between,
   Must serve for ground.

Yes, life advances, till at last
In ice and snow it settles fast,
   A boundless sea—
Caught thus within that cold embrace,
It soon gives up the hopeless race,
   No more to be.

No more for it the halcyon smiles
Of ocean midst its golden isles
    Or inland coves,
Fresh beauty decking happy shores
With gorgeous and exhaustless stores
    Where'er it roves.

Yet once look'd here on thee the fond,
With charms all summer beams beyond,
    Close at thy side;
And now whole worlds, all time and space
That's infinite, with ceaseless pace,
    You both divide!

What contrasts to the cheerful smile
That could the sun himself beguile
    In Eden's bowers;
And this your present frozen state,
Lone, left thus face to face with Fate,
    For future hours!

Well, such is still the lot of man;
So let him bear it as he can,
    And cease to grieve;
If life gave joys that left you fast,
No voice did tell you they would last,
    Or you deceive.

The summer you knew well would fly,
And frigid darkness clothe the sky,
  And barren mould,—
All emblems of your own poor life,
That with its winter must have strife,
  And end in cold.

Just as the cloud at evening tide
With skirts of gold on every side,
  When sinks the ray,—
All stripp'd, must thenceforth, dark and lone,
Through the cold paths of night unknown
  Pursue its way.

This quiet evening on the heart
Now weighs; so rise, and let's depart;
  Necessity
Must be obey'd howe'er we strive;
And even Hope may yet survive,
  With Charity.

Then courage! thought has still a way,
Since youthful gleams can never stay,
  To fly and rise.
Your old companions may be found,
Yes, found, with you still in warmth bound,
  Where nothing dies.

THE LOVER'S WAITING.

THE lightsome ash, by Virgil praised,
　Casts here a chequer'd shade,
Her graceful waving foliage raised
　Midst beech-trees, old, more staid.

She still a sylvan beauty slight,
　And he a friend who tries
To bear loved names for lover's sight,
　Which wanderers surprise.

Youths carve with such a constant mind
　On his smooth, tender bark,
As Orlando of Rosalind
　Would leave on trees the mark.

Such haunting of the forest leaves
　To pour out sentiment,
When no fond fair one it deceives
　Is Love to branches lent.

Oh! be you young or be you old,
　Thus sings a bard of France,
Quite poor, or furnish'd with the gold
　That many will entrance,

If never you have watch'd for feet
    With steps melodious, airy,
At the blue brilliant noontide sweet,
    Like those of some bright fairy—

Of morning's vital alchemy
    Ne'er felt the dewy spell,
While other lips with mystery
    Another's love would tell;

If never you possess'd a heart,
    In one face pure bliss seeing,
If innocence did not impart
    The joy of mingled Being;

If slopes and groves you never saw
    With thoughts of love divine,
Accordant with great Nature's law,
    Another's hand in thine;

If never you have pitied kings,
    For riches felt disdain,
Nought prizing but the pure blest things
    Which make true love remain;

If never yet a woman's eyes
    Could breathe into your soul
Another soul that never dies,
    To constitute a whole;

If never you have wish'd to die
  To save another dear
To you, for whom you ever sigh
  As if she were not near;—

You have not loved. I say no more;
  Unless the angels' wings
Have borne you o'er the earth to soar,
  To breathe their higher things.

Yet these, I think, with grace all mild,
  Will feel no stern contempt
For those who love here, unbeguiled,
  From vice alone exempt.

'Tis but an echo of their voice
  When sages e'en declare
That there can be no better choice
  Than Love's bright hues to wear.

A habitude it is, they prove,
  That's better than all pelf,
To have one near you whom you love
  Far better than yourself.

Thou spirit of sweet human love,
  So soft, and strong, and free,
Hast thou no friends in heaven above
  Who smile with sympathy?

That is a question not for man
　　In this cold darksome clime;
To think and wait is all he can,
　　And leave the rest to time.

Sooth, waiting constitutes our life,
　　Expect—that is the whole;
Yes, such is the insatiate strife
　　Of our still longing soul.

But longing reverie is best,
　　What's present is so small;
Bright hope and patience furnish rest,
　　Joy, peace, content, and all.

While Spring invites our youth to fly,
　　What's distant to behold,
There's one so wrapt with what is nigh,
　　It cannot e'er be told.

But such is nature; love alone
　　Can make each spot so fair!
Imparting an Elysian tone
　　With Tempe's beauty there.

Let others climb the Alpine peak,
　　Through heat to traverse snow.
Why in the summer should we seek
　　What winter did bestow?

Our words in London never froze,
    That you should hear them there,
Dissolving, as some fools suppose,
    Like icicles from hair.

It would be worth their journey slow
    If all we said they knew,
And found it melting, like the snow,
    In love-distilling dew.

Remember'd all too well the cold,
    The tempests, and the sleet,
The pacing on the black, wet mould,
    To wait for fond-loved feet.

Let frozen ridges others seek;
    Here give me summer air,
Where now, amidst some osier creek,
    May peep and smile the fair.

Let France Imperial prize and claim
    Those downs which skirt Savoy,
I know some "slopes" with humble name
    That yield an ample joy.

When seated on a verdant bank
    You wait with hope and fear,
And mark what floated and what sank,
    While bargemen oft would steer;

Watching the leaf slow gliding by,
   And sympathy to feel,
When, to the passing bark too nigh,
   It sinks beneath her keel—

Unsteer'd, abandon'd, to observe
   What soon will be its fate,
While, pensive, wishing it may swerve
   Midst lushy weeds, you wait.

The bridge, that must be pass'd, in sight,
   Attracts your restless eyes;
Though all with flowers round is bright,
   That spot the rest defies.

For one more fair with youthful sheen
   Than May in blossoms new,
Will shortly on that arch be seen
   To prove affection true.

A book you hold with vacant mind;
   You'll turn the page no more;
No poet can your fancy bind,
   With all the Muses' store.

A blade of grass within the leaves
   May rest, and so 'tis well;
Mere waiting now your mind relieves;
   No book has aught to tell.

Oh! watch of Love, "a trance" thou art,
   Say poets sage and true,
Which awes with hope the human heart,
   Though sweet as morning dew.

The hour strikes; still more delay;
   You dread some giant's power;
Or is it sickness makes her stay
   In her mysterious bower?

You know not where, beyond your sight,
   Placed westwards of your way,
Where tints ausonian rest so bright
   Your gaze would ever stay,

Enhancing thus the fragrancy
   Of that which bathes your heart;
Since "knowing not" and mystery
   Can aid Love's gentle part.

Love's secret origin then shown
   To lie in depths so pure,
Since thus you fly to the unknown,
   The vague, and the obscure.

Again another note of time!
   Your fear gives place to dread;
Avaunt, all books of mirth or rhyme!
   Here grief alone is spread.

When lo! that bridge of sighs so late,
    Becomes a rainbow fair;
'Tis not reserved for envious fate
    To cancel what shines there.

'Tis she; that tint remember'd well,
    Disperses all your fear.
Oh! who could now the contrast tell
    When she does thus appear?

See how she steps so light and free,
    No daisy sparkling more,
To fill the heart of man with glee,
    With joy's pure, brightest store!

The spring will buds and florets yield,
    The bank its primrose bright;
But all's eclipsed in woods and field
    When Lizzy bursts to sight.

LONDON.

Ye woods that feel no sun,
    Of animals man-hating, worthy lair,
    Of human things, all bare,
Where grizly boars, and wolves, and badgers run,

Expect the savage man,
    Who strays with dire weapons all to kill,
    And gratify his will;
  Receive not one who much prefers to see
  Bright cities gay and free,
Where children, youths, and maidens gaily ran;

Where Elms old and the Lime,
    Inured to visits from the honey-bee,
    Contented and with glee,
To hear of human voices merry chime,
  Will yield to none of you
    In foliage green and gracious form bright,
    No less a sylvan sight,
    Combined with what will please the feeling
      heart,
  And Love's own arrows dart,
Humanity and Nature in their view.

Shade dreadful, where no ray
    Of cheerful sunlight penetrates thy gloom,
    Of thing half-human tomb,
The " *semi-homo* " shunning wholesome day,—
 Abolish'd is thy rite,
    Which ancient superstition loved of yore,
    Of dreaded Mandragore;
  With no magician now we steal to thee;
  Then lonely ever be;
We envy not thy darksome, spectral night.

Woods with leaves falling now,   [wind,
    And broken branches snapp'd off by the
    What solace can you find
When blasts will pierce and groaning foliage
    bow ?
  A cold and wither'd shade
    Will so invest your fading bowers all,
    Where pale things droop and fall,
  And there stands living nought that can
    remark
  How thou art dull and dark,
And only for some Timon suited, made.

Hence, Thought so solitary,
    With undefined and silent anguish fed,
    In lonely fields first bred—
Where creatures dumb, and sighs, and winds aye
    tarry,
  So restless, rapid still,
    Though flying heedless through material
    things,
    Where lowest nature sings.
  In thy own self still nothing, although all
  Men's deeds spring from thy call—
I hate thy musing, and I ever will.

I hate to hear the shot
    Echoed of men who stray to hurt and kill,
    Or shouts resounding still
Of those whose temper stern, unyielding, hot,

Will burst to awe their dogs
    Through swamps that seem bereft and void
      of soul
    To animate the whole;
  Sounds moving in a hoarse, harsh way, phan-
    tasmal,
  Unmeaning, ever dismal
As the dull chant of marsh-infesting frogs.

There loathed lethargy,
    Save to the senses, wishing to forget,
    Forgetting, and to let
Matter rule all things, and sole potent be,
  Reigns still beneath such shade,
    Where music's rapture is a thing unknown,
    As if men heartless grown,
  Where no one seems to borrow any light
  Beyond mere bestial sight,
Should never ask of Genius her bright aid.

  But come, thou spirit ever gay,
  Which mildly can our London sway;
  Where thought, endued with healthy tone,
  Will feed not on herself alone;
  A mental naked wilderness,
  Where emptiness will hearts oppress;
  As in the crowds that vaguely see
  The ocean's vast immensity,
  You might too add with contemplation,
  But that their thoughts still nothing rest on;

                      P

So merely fix'd there, like a plant,
To gaze all day, or else to rant
About some interest they expect
Which can no ray of heaven reflect—
Come thence to where the motley crowd
Has nothing vague within to shroud,
But finds a varied banquet spread
To satisfy each heart and head,
From things majestic, holy, grand,
To what is slight, and sweet, and bland,
From rites uniting heaven with earth
To sports and songs of harmless mirth.
While rustic scenes yield earthly sound,
Here heaven's own golden harps seem found,
As if by Haydn or Mozart
In holy rites to fill a part,
When souls by women's voices raised
Know in their depths that God is praised ;
Or by those masters old, unknown,
Who to the plain-chant gave that tone
Which floats resistless round the soul
With power unrivall'd reigning sole—
Though heard but for a moment's space,
Yet leaving what time can't efface—
Those solemn sounds that never vary,
As of the deep, wild Miserere ;
When plaintive depths of spirit feel
What no tongue mortal can reveal—
As if by some angelic might
Still causing all that comes in sight

To fade away and disappear
While those repeated tones you hear.

London has seen her cruel days;
But they have pass'd; good-humour stays.
Intolerance elsewhere may linger,
But here none point a scornful finger;
While we breathe liberty, that air
In daily life alone found there.
For here, sooth, men are apt to learn
What in the fields they can't discern—
On neutral ground to meet the age,
And no vain contest with it wage—
To take a wide and lofty view
Of much that wears an aspect new;
To know that others would have loved
The things from which they were removed
By difference of times and age,
As living in an earlier stage
Of Christian social instincts grand,
Form'd by their nature to expand—
That what they did not live to see,
They would have loved like you and me;
Have wished, like any in the crowd
(Though voices now may sound more loud),
To hail what serves humanity;
And deem it nought but charity—
To cherish thoughts both deep and grand,
No true good feeling to withstand;

To know that times can often be
When kindness is best policy,
No prudence even to compare
With views unselfish, that will dare
Do all things generous to prove
Great confidence in people's love.
And though Plutocracy sweeps by,
There still is more equality
Than in the rustic field or crowd,
Where Fashion yields to Dulness proud,
As if replies both cold and gruff
Denoted liberty enough;
While here the lowly, bright, and gay,
Content, pursue their smiling way,
And treading on each other's heels,
Disdain for any no one feels,
Unruffled each, though grandeur nigh,
With all appendages, you spy,
That heartless, tasteless, witless throng,
Where genius must be always wrong;
Books, pictures, friends—all nothing there;
But an epergne will make them stare.
Though files like these you must disdain,
Of nought else seen you will complain.
For each one here regard must pay
To those who come across his way;
And as for dull, grim, gloomy pride,
The very stones would it deride.
Guide blind men 'cross the street, says Gay;
But what did one I guided say?

" *Thank you, Miss,*" yet much I spoke ;
My pay was thus a first-rate joke,
At which my friends all laugh'd and shouted,
Esteeming I was hugely flouted.
So kindly acts oft end in fun,
And furnish mirth when day is done.
Frank and good-natured, sharp, yet kind,
Becomes the true-bred London mind ;
A laugh will often then supply
The place of a censorious eye.
That mind contracts unfeign'd respect
For much where others scorn affect ;
With all its love for highest truth,
It flies not at the face of youth ;
Unlike the ancient Garden school,
It would let Love with goodness rule.
Unlike the new Parisian mind,
To many failings it is blind ;
" *The ill that is of women said*"
To six editions there has led ;
The same pen then " *their good*" would tell ;
But the production did not sell.
In London books like these would be
Quite sure just the reverse to see.
Though we detest pedantic ways
Of loving or of giving praise,
It finds a certain dignity
In all pure muliebrity,
Mere individual that shows
Like the slight lily or the rose,

With sweetness such as fairest flowers
Impart to brightest earthly bowers.
And what if fashion reigns around?
Don't flowers aid it from their ground?
Yea, they e'en pass beyond us there
If girls with florets you compare.
For there is the Hybiscus vain,
Of whom no botanists complain;
Her colour changing thrice a day,
Is not that, then, an instance, pray?
Her morning-dress is simply white;
At noon with pink she is bedight;
And in the evening deepest red
She wears, thus by her Fashion led.
Our beauties are not like these flowers
So mutable through each day's hours.
Although, like Flora with her clock,
Their hours may oft your habits shock,
Like certain Yuccas, which seem made
Still chiefly for the night and shade;
Coming thus forth with beauty bright
Yet only in the pale moonlight,
As Heliotropes prefer the sun,
Beneath whose beams their course is run.
For plants strange hours oft will keep,
While other flowers are asleep.
There are who blow from midnight all
Till four or five, at Nature's ball;
And, like us, too, this kind of rage
Depends upon the parties' age;

As Trefoil, when quite young, will sleep
When elder petals vigils keep,
Still closing sooner in the night,
As for such tender things is right.
Diurnal and nocturnal states
Will differ thus without debates,
According to the age of each,
Which can or cannot Fashion reach ;
And Fashion's clock, like Flora's too,
Hangs open to the public view ;
For some will peep out quite betimes,
When hearing first the church's chimes ;
At seven, or eight, or nine, or ten,
Like Vicoïde Napolitain,
Souci des Champs, and many more,
Still just as in the days of yore.
But some can only leave their room
Much later, when the Œillets bloom ;
When half at least the day is gone,
They come forth like Léontodon.
Still let us not condemn or judge,
But leave them, when they can, to trudge.
Then parties all in blue and pink
Proclaim the sun about to sink—
Parties we say, for who can tell
The angel that keeps by them well ?
While others first, like Belle de Nuit,
At five (not earlier) you see.
London of course has other clocks ;
But some choose these of auburn locks,

Of bonnets, pretty hats so small,
(Not long grim hands upon a wall ;)
They go by, frocks of every hue,
Which " the right time " announce to you ;
Even although you be like him
Who had not studied women's whim,
Who neither knew, nor would pretend
To know, although he was their friend,
About them aught, or their concerns ;
Though from them, thus, the time one learns.

Then, too, what oft excites disdain,
And of which foreigners complain,
Combines, I think, with Fashion here
To make our London Beauty dear ;
Since its slight finery, like flowers,
Requiring no portentous dowers,
Evinces innocence in glee
Which yields a true delight to see ;
Such contrasts showing to the proud,
Who would their wealth proclaim aloud
By high-priced things, which, after all,
Oft yield in beauty to the small.

In London hearts become so wise
That subtlest truths they recognize ;
They know, like notes which music aid,
For one another we are made ;
No discord, though unlike is each
To those above, below his reach.

Then simple ways, in either sex,
In town no genius ever vex ;
And, intimate with lowly youth,
You learn to trust in other's truth ;
As they will answer yes or no,
Esteeming each thing simply so—
A feeling which must prove most strange
To those before confined to range
Amidst the self-thought polish'd host
Who of their county greatness boast.

So all things common here are found
As sweet as light and love around.
Bright, joyous spirit, arch and witty,
Yet ever prompt the poor to pity,
And seeing in each low condition
Still daily motives for compassion,
Oh! come and teach us aye to find
Some way ingenious to be kind.
Come and unite us to the fold
Which genius loved in times of old,
Where Shakspeare studied, Dryden sung,
Observing still the old and young.
Where once lived Knights of great Saint
     John,
Of whom the memory is gone,
True heroes, poets, leaving still
Majestic traces of their will,
Like vestures to adorn the scene
If naked weakness intervene.

Unlike old Athens in her pride,
That no great men could long abide,
When Chabrias to Egypt fled,
Timotheus wise to Lesbos sped,
Conon in Cyprus left his name,
Iphicrates to Thracia came,
Our London ne'er beheld the bard
Who found her treatment of him hard—
The hero whom she forced to fly,
Or even whom she would decry,
The victim of oppressors near,
For whom she did not yield a tear;
For all the crimes she ever knew
Were wrought by foes, a hostile crew.
Come then and witness glorious sites,
Where cruel record each invites—
Where More and Fisher nobly died,
Undaunted by a tyrant's pride,
That we might never discords feel
Such as still present times reveal;
Where Faith will pass from hand to hand
The torch which tempests can withstand,
Transmitting still that holy flame
Without which all's an empty name;
Where Heaven's majestic truths once more
Will yield unutterable store
Of peace and gladness to the crowd,
Recoiling from the false and proud.
Haste thee, glad Spirit, soft and strong,
And let me hear thy dulcet song,

Revealing all the treasures deep
That in our London depths we reap,
Which has its wrecks that poets grieve,
But still more calms that don't deceive,
Its peaceful hours so blithe and gay,
Its foamless isles where halcyons stay,
Like bowers of the purple East,
Where we can have the wileless feast
Of conversation tender, holy,
Dispelling all dull melancholy,
As when our Herbert, thoughtful, wise,
Points westward to the evening skies,
Dissolved in wordless converse there,
Fann'd by bright plumes of evening air,
Or to deep subtle talk descending,
Like some true sage the hours spending;
Enjoying Fancy's lofty dream,—
Himself, in truth, what others seem,
In his sweet garden's sunny nook
Teaching things highest by his look,—
Deep truths that words cannot express,
But clothed in Art's most glorious dress;
Leading back those you once loved near
By his kind word and starting tear;
By talk that might old Time arrest,
And give impatient spirits rest,
While bending with great Nature's power
Within his magic sunny bower
A shroud of thoughts to hide him there
From what is vulgar in the air,—

A mockery both proud and base
Of what in life he loves to trace ;
Yes, come and still defy the proud
Who would not sing such themes aloud ;
As if when we can't high worth see
We practise most humility,
Most decorum, and most fine tact,
Because we sing no glorious fact.

Come, gracious Spirit, all this tell,
And we at least respond, 'Tis well.
Then, leaving Art's beloved domains,
Pass to where Faith with Priesthood reigns.

Tell of the sages grave and mild
Who wait upon the outcast child ;
Tell of him, aye, the poor man's friend,
Who time and life itself will spend,
Still seeking chiefly what's within,
And heeding not the former sin,
To raise those fallen poorest there
Above all earth's infected air,
Until each truly lives and sings,
And envies not the wealth of kings.
Come, let me feel the ancient spells
Of which our Edward fondly tells ;
Hearing old truths unfolded till
To combat them he lost the will,
In grave De Bure and Merlin's trace
Finding unconsciously his place.

With Toulouse too, that type so bland,
As if he could not truth withstand,
He sinks, resistless, to the mould
Which fashion'd all these men of old,
And shows how London need not yield
To Paris in his special field.
No sceptic who to doubts has pander'd,
Though you might read upon his standard,
As by Lucretius signified,
That " souls are pious, dignified,
When they regard all things they see
With patient sweet tranquillity [1]."
He yet allows e'en fools to find
In him an inconsistent mind,
From wanting only that decision
Which makes men take their right position.
Intensely delicate and keen,
Insensible to worldly sheen ;
With sympathizing heart for all,
That spies and waits for no one's call,
Giving sweet dainties in the streets
To each poor ragged child he meets,
He makes still many hope that he
May be led home by Charity,
To light supernal, safest way,
From which at last he will not stray.

Then pass we to the garden bowers,
Where Nature is all prankt with flowers,

[1] Sed mage placata posse omnia mente tueri.

Where birds, though all the crumbs are spent,
Still haunt parterres with merriment,
On soft aërial kisses fed,
While hopping near you without dread.
Let Paris boast Elysian Fields—
I know a spot which all that yields,
Where marble vases brightly crown'd
With all that ever deck'd a ground,
And zephyrs over florets playing,
As at the dawn of day awaking,
Transport Italian scenes to home,
And leave us with no wish to roam.
There gay amidst the sportive crowd
Of boys and children shouting loud,
Of youth serene, with ways and looks
That make insipid mirthful books,
You look on things with certain eyes
Which see beyond some counted wise.
" Thus childhood," says a sage acute,
" For Faith seems half a substitute ;"
And London is the place to find
A childhood suited to that mind.
In these fair gardens you forget
That on which elsewhere thoughts are set ;
Your mind, dismissing sorrows past,
Is fill'd with love Lethean vast,
And gains at once so bright a tone
It cannot feel itself alone,
In silence speaking with the eye
To all who near you saunter by.

For yours the charm of strange device
To strike up friendship in a trice ;
While speaking with a certain tone
You mingle all hearts with your own.
For gentle meaning of your looks
Speaks better things than any books.
Then strangers prove best company,
Yourself no longer solitary ;
For solitude, that once oppress'd,
Is here not vacancy, but rest ;
Aërial merriment around,
Dull gloom avoids such cheerful ground.

But now hear London's special boast—
What pleases foreign Christians most ;
The Mediæval Sunday here
Still proves itself in life most dear ;
The ancient Canons, yet in force,
Are found to yield the best resource—
Industrious channels multiplied,
And yet the clergy edified.
The sophist wonders and complains ;
The Day of Rest for all remains ;
No Scotch fanaticism known ;
Yet no result Parisian grown.
If our museums all are closed,
The evil is not what's supposed ;
Grim Science loves to show and talk,
But youth prefers to play and walk.

If painted pictures it can't see,
Each will himself a picture be,
Will care to show a neat, smart dress,
That can a cheerful mind express.
But what can better strength repair
Than strolls through parks and gardens fair?
And what can better teach the mind
Than gentle converse with our kind?
Companions cheerful, pleasing, free,
Forming bright bands of chivalry,
Untaught too oft in humble life,—
But never with the Church at strife?
While Godless banners are unfurl'd,
Here's an example for the world,
To prove how interests all agree
With ancient, true Divinity.

And then, in London we have peace;
With loyal concord, combats cease.
Our " *Demonstrations* " are but few,
And those confined but to a crew
That with good meaning, seldom rough,
Find one such day is quite enough.
As elsewhere, there are monsters low,
But them you are not forced to know.
No bastions, four great streets commanding,
Are there arranged for armies standing,
Whence soldiers can direct cross-fire
To make all strategists admire

The corner dangerous and fell,—
Devised, constructed, kept so well,
'Gainst new ideas and subversive
Which to pass that way would now strive;
We saunter on and feel no fear,
Though vellum thunder may be near,
To keep up just appearances,
With music and endearances,
That boys and maidens there may find
Some pastime suited to their mind.
'Tis true that some here boast a Press
Which wears the Revolution's dress,
Though somewhat modified indeed,
Not openly distrusts to breed;
But while belonging to that school
Subservient to its wide-spread rule,
Its cant and falsehoods using well
Which elsewhere prove sure means to sell—
To have its pages in each hand
Is what its adepts can't command.
Whole tribes, in fact, the great unknown,
Its secret projects all disown.
These never can, in truth, conceive
That men with phrases would deceive.
The few contract the foreign pest;
The many, who read least, have rest.
So, while the scribes would mischief find,
The crowd has quite another mind.
'Tis peace all day and peace by night,
With nought that can the Muses fright.

Q

I know what 'tis at early dawn
To hear the din of battles drawn,
Convulsing all the air with thunder,
To see men pale with rage and wonder;
I can well therefore praise the spot
Where glories such as these are not.
Here at each dawn we bless the sun,
Its sweet kind course prepared to run
Untroubled by the shock of arms,
By dread, which all our projects harms.
If these are gifts that you disdain,
Fly elsewhere by the swiftest train;
But leave me here, to see combined
All things that on the earth we find
To render happy mortal life,
And moderate its woes and strife.

But to pursue our common way,
For wiser tongues may all this say.
So back unto the park we stroll
With book in hand on grass to roll;
There, when you would salute the dawn,
And brush with feet the dewy lawn,
You stumble on no ancient spell
Working out death, for some to tell
In that great Marshal's polish'd way,
When Bolingbroke to mortal fray
Call'd Norfolk out, and all he said
Was, " Let some officers be sped

To whom we may the rest consign
How to direct their *fair design*[3]."
But sweet Good-Humour on a throne,
To whom all there will homage own,
Presiding free we find each hour,
And no one eye or lip to lour.
Then slopes, a couch of green and gold,
Receive the gentle, young and old,
Where murmuring music floats along,
Commingled with the thrush's song,
And boats and barges slowly glide
By a bright spangled emerald side,
While cheerful voices ring around,
And no grim solitude is found;
But living beauty in its shrine
Can make you feel its soul divine—
Make you reflect on secret sorrow
Till from it all you goodness borrow—
Make you e'en just excuses find
For some whom sweet seductions bind;
While each kind thought within responds
To Nature's universal bonds.
For wit, and art, and wisdom deep,
Will mental riches thereby reap;
And these, methinks, without pretence,
Are sympathies of soul and sense—
Knowing that in God's gracious sight
The human heart is often right;

[3] Shakspeare, Richard II.

While pedants and your stern declaimer
Will ever try their best to shame her.
Unmark'd above, no sigh, no tear
Can pass, although neglected here.
The Heart Divine will never sleep;
It watches those on earth who weep;
And midst the bold, bad, busy throng,
It knows those who to Love belong,
Whose gladness amidst dire privation
Sheds radiance on the lowest station,
When struggles, songs, and tuneful tears
Are heard amidst symphonious spheres;
Where unseen sorrows sound most sweet,
Ascending from the gayest street;
Since there the anguish and the din
Prepare a crown for what's within.

Through peopled haunts of human kind
You pass, and to their failings blind;
Like that fair witch who watch'd the sleep
Of mortals, and with kindness deep
Still drew from it a pleasure sweet,
Perhaps for angels not unmeet,
While seeing through their rude disguise,
And with serene, forgiving eyes,
The naked beauty of the soul,
Which constitutes in truth the whole
Of what, as in a summer bower,
Gives life to many a starry flower.

It is a thought of common sense,
However, some would chase it hence,
That we are like the angels all,
Or else like demons in their fall,—
The last comparatively few,
If only the whole truth we knew;
The former, past expression kind,
No music softer than their mind!
Though face, and looks, and winning ways,
Suffice to show where Goodness stays,—
And Goodness, thinking itself hidden,
Contented to be daily chidden,
Still thinking its perfume unknown,
Though nought on earth is like its own.
Some will now call this all excess,
Mere stuff to make a poet's dress.
But no; here's no Utopian talk;
'Tis with an artist's eye to walk,
Without which men are blind as moles
While ranting about hearts and souls.

Thus, straying through the London street,
A halo rests on those you meet;
While yielding still to hope and mirth,
To gloom your brooding gives no birth.
But all things lovelier appear
Reflected from what must be dear,—
A thousand pleased and pleasing eyes,
Which cast a light that can surprise;

Whilst nods, and becks, and wreathèd smiles
Can play, and fear no fatal wiles.

Then through tall snow-like columns long
The warm winds catch the minstrel's song.
Or pictures, books, and statues fair
Create a true poetic air,　　.
Which leaves you little to lament,
Though on the country minds were bent.

Or would you seek to be more free?
You speed to shades of greenwood-tree;
To the bright, lawny, gracious slope
Which bounds for many youthful hope,
To tangled glens, and meadows small,
Wood-embosom'd amidst them all;
For London is the nurse of Taste
Which oft to mossy banks will haste.
Mere country folks can rarely spy
The charm of brook, or copse, or sky;
While him who in the City pants,
Each smallest rural thing enchants.
Then Norwood, Hampstead, draw you on
To range through oaks till day is gone.
Then Beulah's garden serves for port
When with a friend you would resort
To benches that will front the West,
Where you can talk, or sing, and rest;
Or on the lush grass roll so free,
When the wind bends it gracefully.

Or would you with the flowing tide
From Chelsea upwards row or glide?
Then Twickenham, with its fairy isle,
Could marvellously hours beguile;
As Kew and Richmond, bright with green,
Have often pleased you with their sheen,
When wander'd on the sparkling wave
The airs so sweet which evening gave;
While near you ever as you stray
The sportive youth is seen to play;
Or, in the old Athenian mode,
You seek Thermopolist's abode;
For in the classic page we find
Of cups like ours a certain kind [4],
Which Rome accepted when she sold
Mere water hot or mixtures cold
To blend with herbs that served for tea,
Such as refreshes you and me,
Till a proud Emperor forbad
That such delights should there be had;
For Claudius, with despotic pride,
Would have no more of it supplied.

Thus London all sweet joys can yield,
Those even of the wood and field—
The scenes of pastoral delight,
Arcadia brought of all in sight,

[4] Philemon.

While the next hour you can be
Amidst the din or harmony
Of streets, and halls that suit the fair,
While only harmless mirth is there.
You've town and country all in one—
An instant, and from each you're gone.

Then, when draws on the sober night,
There's much that still awaits the sight;
For cities' moonlit spires stand
In solitude sublime and grand,—
And see these garlands, star with star,
To guide your feet that wander far;
Where order, as in Nature wide,
Will seem to yield on every side;
And not as when man seeks to deck
With brilliancy some little speck,
Arranged, complete with symmetry;
Whereas, what is divine will be
Scatter'd, unravell'd, seeming then
Confusion to the eyes of men,—
An emblem, as sage Bacon shows,
Of truth, which man but dimly knows,
In broken fragments, here and there,
For human order with no care.
Nature's spirit is so unlike
The lights which human spirits strike;
Though here these stars, thus up and down,
Through all the mazes of the town,

Seem lost in labyrinths of gold
O'er plains cerulean, manifold ;
Like planets in confusion strange
Through which the milky-way will range ;
Though squares, triangles, still you trace,
As through the heaven's vaulted space
Through floods of interstellar air
Of sapphire deep past all compare.

But now no time can here be spared,
Such banquets are for mind prepared,
Where all degrees, in mighty throng,
Repair to the abodes of song,
Or to the stage, where, fancy free,
They witness all so thoughtfully.
There soft sweet Lydian airs recall
The theme which most delighteth all,
With music's own omnipotence,
The soul so mingles with the sense !
Or the high Tragic Muse appears,
At whose command will flow the tears
Of those whose feelings now unfold
Thoughts that lay deep, till then untold.
For what more delicate and fine
Than the crowds there who can combine
With such true taste ideal life
And their own real daily strife ?
The plebs of Livy, mob of Burke,
Are not grown harden'd by their work.

No delicacy can surpass
The sense of beauty in the mass.
No sympathy is wanting here,
No deep compassion with its tear;
And when the true sublime is found,
Enthusiasm reigns around.
And what is that but probity?
A poet asks, but honesty?
'Tis there, from ranks the lowest down,
That Genius finds its noblest crown—
A woman's cry, a woman's tears,
Before sweet Desdemona's fears;
For Arthur's woes, a mother's cry,
A mother's deep and long-drawn sigh;
Before great Hamlet's inky stole,
The cry of a deep human soul.

This people from the London streets
Can still admire all it meets.
Like the great Bard, this crowd can see
In Genius hospitality.
It enters, wond'ring, hat in hand,
To love its host and understand.
Whatever critics may pretend,
Here dull mistrust and doubts will end.
The crowd, determin'd to admire,
In praising genius will not tire.
It finds all perfect to its heart—
The most condemn'd, suspected part,

It picks up, carries all away,
Through all the streets it then must stray.
No word of beauty it will miss,
It has no other wit but this.
So pensive or delighted, wild,
Each grown a hero or a child,
Removed above the tedious coil
Amidst which they must often toil,
They leave the scene transported then,
More soft, and therefore wiser men,
To feel within their conscience blest,
And yield to Nature's call to rest.

Then let all others blame and scorn;
These crowds at least are not forlorn;
For every item in the whole
Of human nature and the soul
That can the smallest object be
Of God's great love, in each degree
Is here discover'd, traced, and found,
And varied, with no limits bound.

So Truth and Beauty, Goodness, here
Complete a happy atmosphere,
Still fairer than the sun can see,
Inspiring all mysteriously.
For God can ever counteract
Your sophist race, and that's a fact.

Since these delights our London yields,
Let others haunt the lonely fields.
Let others all her faults assemble;
To me such critics but resemble
Those who the Himalayas rake,
Their inventory try to make;
Accomplish'd men of science grown
For having parted stone from stone.
Let Etna vomit lava, flame,
Grave men like these are still the same.
For pinch by pinch its dust they try,
While light flies upwards to the sky.

Let each one choose his special way,
But I would with the poet [5] say,
That, like an animal, I gaze,
And only feel a blank amaze.
That's why of London now I sung,
And with a eulogistic tongue.
But good to see, and to admire
With true enthusiastic fire,
And in our times all this to tell,
Who knows?   Perhaps it may be well.

[5] V. Hugo.

THE POET'S VOCATION.

THE leaves and flowers lately bright,
Methinks seem seized with sudden fright.
A rising wind approaching near
With shadows, can explain their fear.
The floret bends its gentle head;
The leaf prepares to fly with dread;
A far commotion in the air
Thus changes what was erst so fair.
This morn, with sunshine glad around,
All sweet, soft, soothing things were found;
While now the thoughtless can discern
That Nature has her lessons stern,
Which sometimes we should like as well
As when she waves bright Pleasure's spell.

But hark! a foreign minstrel's song [1],
Whose sweet wild air delights the throng.

If oft they say the Muse's wing
Should only stale ambrosia fling

[1] Partly translated from the French.

O'er all she passes by,
Yield merely sweetness idly spread,
To lull a soft unthinking head,
    Oh! heed not what they cry.

Ye poets, sacred and sublime,
Oh! hasten in your souls to climb
Wild northern summits clad in snow,
To rest on holy plains below,
To woods where autumn winds will rave,
To vales where sleeps the tranquil wave,
Where Nature spreads a landscape fair,
Where to green pastures flocks repair,
Where goats will nibble fragrant flowers,
Where ancient arcades yield their bowers
For the young shepherds, seated, singing;
While evening zephyrs, freshness bringing,
Lash with bright cascades o'er the steeps
The dark splash'd rock that ever weeps.
Wherever feathers soar and fly,
Where'er are plains or mountains high,
Old forests with their boughs that moan,
Parch'd isles or lakes deserted, lone;
Green hills, park, moor, or land, or wave,
Wherever the four winds can rave,
Where setting suns prolong the shade
Of oaks, or verdant slopes are made
By undulating chains of ground,
Wherever field and corn are found,

Where'er hangs fruit from bough that sinks,
Wherever bird the dewdrop drinks,
There suspend your azure wing,
Rest, and, while beholding, sing.

Speed to the woods, to vales profound,
And hearken to each passing sound;
Let isolated notes produce
A concert for your special use;
In Nature seek, thus rudely spread,
And, whether full of joy or dread,
In spring and summer, cheerful, bright,
In winter, gloomy to the sight—
The word mysterious, ever near
To him who lends attentive ear,
How it is God who filleth all
Beneath His solemn living pall,
The world His temple, in which sings
With joy each of created things;
One, and alone, He rules the world,
His glory beaming and unfurl'd,
In the star and in the flower—
In the perfume of the bower!

Drink, drink! and to inebriation—
Ye poets, this is your vocation—
The grass, the brook, the restless leaves,
The distant scene that fancy weaves,
When thinking that she hears by night
The voice of pilgrims hid from sight,

The first pale florets that surprise
February's awaking eyes,
The water, air, and barren field,
The sound monotonous that yield
Huge waggons grinding through the wood,
Slow dragg'd along with tott'ring hood.

Ye eagle's brothers love the hills
When tempests swell the mountain rills,
When sombre clouds obscure the space,
And tracks and objects all efface,
Hurling vast shatter'd trees to lean
O'er tall wild rocks with gulfs between.

When morning gilds the brilliant air,
Oh, think what purity is there!
As mists sweep o'er the sloping lawn,
And dazzling brightness follows dawn;
The woods half hidden by the light
Which rises from the womb of night,
The orb effulgent mounting higher,
Like some vast dome that would aspire
To send its cupola of gold
Above the clouds with art so bold;
As when approaching them we see
Piles oriental blissfully.
Drink likewise at the evening hours,
When shadows close o'er Nature's bowers,
The landscape, now become obscure,
No forms displaying plain or sure,

All roads and rivers half effaced,
Horizons sharply to be traced
By hills which look like giants there
On elbows resting in their lair,
Stretch'd out while lost in revery
Each uncouth figure seems to be.
If thus of images should roll,
Living, and press'd within your soul,
An inward world, with deepest thought
And sentiments that spring unsought,
Of ardent passion, and of love
To fructify the world above—
Then blend it quickly, constantly,
With the whole universe you see,
Which visibly surrounds you here;
So be to all creation dear.
For oh! ye poets wise and holy,
Know that your art sublime is wholly,
It is that deep, mysterious sound,
Simple yet diverse, high, profound,
Resistless as the speeding wave
That onward sweeps when torrents rave,
Echoed by all created things,
With which the whole of nature rings;
Be skilful, then, to strike each chord,
That God on earth be well adored.

CLISSON.

WHAT scatter'd hosts, long on the wane,
Come drifting o'er the sombre plain,
Though woods that line the wind-blown road
Last evening were their loved abode!
The western gusts, unseen, while nigh,
Impel leaves thus like ghosts to fly,
Driven as by enchanter's spell,
All pale and dead, with much to tell.

It was a dark autumnal day
When first to Clisson I would stray;
The groves were clad in brown and green,
To suit the interval between
The parting friend and coming foe
So sure to lay their beauties low.
Thick hedge-rows, groves, and small rich fields,
The region that surrounds it yields;
Methought I spied at each brake pass
The peasants risen in a mass,
Entrench'd within the pathless wood,
Where hostile legions were withstood
By rustics all like heroes now,
With sacred cause and holy vow.

But changed abruptly all I found,
Descending o'er a rugged ground;
Until I reach'd a deep ravine,
The Sèvre winding on between;
When suddenly there raised its head,
All spectral-like, quite causing dread,
The vast huge Pile, so dark and hoary,
Whose chequer'd fame aye lives in story,
While stretch'd along and at its feet
I saw the village winding street
Far scatter'd up and down, and strange;
Just such as on some Alpine range
Will lead you to the welcome spot
Where soon fatigues are all forgot.

Long grass-grown steps cut o'er the rock
Which shelves down in a mighty block
Conduct you to the portals grand
Which green with ivy proudly stand.
There now, within these crumbling walls,
Lives recent Fame that pity calls,
When standing o'er that fatal well
Down whose dark depths the victims fell,
Who fought to stay an impious hand
And cruel despots to withstand.
Then on I stray'd through towers vast
That now stand open to the blast,
All roofless, split on every side,
Where owls and bats can well abide,

Such canopies of creeping flowers
Combine with walls to make their bowers,
Through courts where huge trees cast a shade
As in some haunted forest glade,
Through many a grim spacious room
Where all is desolation, gloom ;
Each window still with iron barr'd,
As suiting manners stern and hard,
If possible, more dreary still,
From such left traces of the skill
Which fashion'd all things that you see,
If not for pain, with mystery.

So musing, through these rooms I pass'd,
Expecting each would prove the last,
Till lost in mazes without end,
Alone, unguided, with no friend,
I thought I might for ever stray,
And backward never find my way ;
Ah, me ! what 'tis to feel alone
And listen so to Nature's moan !
So vast, intricate is the Pile,
That easily it might beguile
And lead the stranger to some cell
Whence soon emerge he could not well,
Such yawning pitfalls all around,
And branches thick with creepers bound,
At least if night approach'd to close
A scene where novel are no woes.

For ruins fearful so, I ween,
In no place elsewhere I had seen.
My own ancestral ruin'd wall
Is nothing to these towers tall.

Yet here first came to find his nest
The good Crusader, seeking rest.
This Oliver, surnamed the Old,
To help Jerusalem was bold ;
Till, wearied with all war at length,
And feeling weak remains of strength,
He wish'd to spend the rest of life
Removed from every mortal strife.
He found these woods, this stream so fair,
He chose to build his castle there ;
Which then breath'd only rest and peace,
For which from arms he sought release.
So he who Palestine had trod
Lived here absorb'd in love of God.
Those blessed acres he had seen,
Both French and English knights between,
All fighting for a noble cause
Which great Saint Louis thither draws,
Immortal titles to his crown
Thus adding, ne'er to be laid down,
As Norfolk wish'd for England's king,
When Shakspeare would our Richard sing.
Obedient therefore to the light
That shone within his soul, our knight

Proceeded in that company
To prove his glorious chivalry;
Not like some spendthrifts now who roam
Because they hate to live at home.
To knights of old their homes were dear;
Witness poor Joinville's falling tear;
But they left what did charm their eyes
To offer God its sacrifice.
But when his age did now recall
Him to repair to rafter'd hall,
He chose this site, where he could see
Sweet Peace with just Prosperity.

Behold him then pursuing still
The instincts of his honest will,
Straying by the bright gliding river,
Or through green woods where leaflets quiver.
By meads where Sèvre gently flow'd,
So thoughtfully he often rode;
There, resting on the moss-grown stone,
He liked to find himself alone,
While, seated in some cool recess,
He drank in all its quietness.
Oft there he laid his languid head
Midst scatter'd leaves and nothing said;
Though while his limbs lay on the brink,
He own'd a heart that could not sink;
So high, and winged, and cheerful then,
Were all these wise heroic men.

In tranquil wand'rings thus he sought
Great God, for whom he lived and fought,
All Europe to defend with arms,
The Church to shield from war's alarms;
For how could he unmoved behold
Polluted by the Turk so bold
The holy city, ever dear,
Where Christ Himself had shed a tear?
So, though his heart was set on peace,
Jerusalem he would release.
But now that vision all was o'er,
And he must seek another shore—
Those shores eternal where he'd see
That Lord he loved so tenderly.

Oh! solemn traces of the past,
And destined for some few to last—
We needs must pause beneath thy wall,
And things gone by in heart recall—
Weep thy poor wrecks, as o'er a grave,
Of base oblivion's present wave.

But now behold an alter'd scene
As fresh events will intervene;
For here great Constables of France
Through feudal towers will advance.
This holy and serene abode,
Through which the old Crusader strode,
Must now be fenced and fortified,
Since nearer foes must be defied.

No more from distant wars alone
These lofty towers take their tone ;
On every side entrenchments new
Present the strength that now we view,
Which Francis, named " the Second," king,
Will then to its completion bring.
For thither oft will he resort
To hold high revels with his court.
But scenes like these I would pass o'er,
Denoting evil oft of yore.
It is a mingled time of strife,
Not purely of heroic life.
The world shows there its sullied banner
Just in its old and heartless manner.
High grandeur, goodness if you will,
Are there—but with corruption still—
Struggles importing, mean, obscure,
Not Fame for ever to endure.
A waning faith, a doubtful king—
O'er such the Muse will flap her wing,
And soar beyond, elsewhere to find
Themes more congenial to her mind.
From towers such she takes her flight,
And leaves them to the silent night
Of time, which dooms them soon to be
A sign of mutability.
Their latest glory was to shine
To shelter a Rochejacquelin,
When that heroic noble dame,
Chose danger, not a life of shame ;

Her presence casting one last ray
To finish Clisson's glorious day.

But now the night drew on apace;
And homeward tracks I had to trace,
Mere wrecks and ruins leaving all,
And no one caring when they fall.
With loud discordant cries uprose
Hoarse ravens, jackdaws, rooks, and crows,
Whose sable flight obscured the air
Where once reposed the gay and fair;
These flocks above would still remain,
As if to eye their proud domain,
All cawing, croaking, one by one,
A thing to watch and ponder on—
Though you reject old history,
And will not heed a mystery
Such as the crows of Gevaudan
When legendary rumours ran.

Through oceans wild the race of men
Did seem to me as moving then—
A sea unfathom'd, where must lie
All those who were born but to die—
As poets sing, where waves are years,
Aye brackish with our human tears,
Though sick of prey, yet howling on,
As in the ages dead and gone.
But wrecks like the majestic Past,
Gigantic, seldom now are cast

On its inhospitable shore,
However it may rage for more.
'Tis fragments of a smaller world
That chiefly on the rocks are hurl'd;
While infinitely little things,
Such as the storm now stranded flings
For future men to analyze,
Will fill them with a sad surprise;
Since microscopic morals all,
Unlike material objects small,
More worthless prove the more they show,
And smaller still the more you know.
Dark treachery and egotism
You can't make bright by any prism.
Faith, justice, honour, all defied,
Will not more please when magnified;
Compliance cool, non-intervention,
Of no outrageous crime prevention,
You can't make fair by any glass
Through which their foul contents you pass.
The heeding not a nation's cries
For justice,—heeding but supplies
To feather well one's private nest,
Is but a sorry sight at best.
From things like these no dazzling blaze,
No forms all gracious to amaze,
No Alps of sapphire, opal chains,
Sahara's crystals, emerald veins—
No light from the celestial space
Of Isis' festive wondrous trace;

But uglier the more you see,
Grown hideous to mystery,
These wrecks will shock the more you think,
Till in oblivion's depths they sink.
Yet fragments such, I own, produce
A consequence of highest use.
They may be studied with effect;
They now may force men to reflect;
While infinitely small create
Sensations infinitely great,
Meet food for most insatiate thought,
Now by the same waves ever brought,
As pulverized and dash'd on shore,
Each tide will spread them more and more.

LUZANÇAY.

WHAT means this boast of ever-green,
As if on earth were lasting sheen?
Methinks that some who make it here
Betray some indexes of fear.
They do not, quite so proudly fair,
Uplift their points to autumn air.
Deep nestling in a darksome shade,
They seem to court no clear parade.
I can detect some turning brown,
As if with stain'd and faded gown;

Some, even split, and black, and curl'd,
Seem downwards likely to be hurl'd;
Though, as unwilling to be seen,
They shrink behind the others green.
Well, it is cruelty to spy
So sharply as we pass them by.
We owe them somewhat of a debt
For hinting they would never let
The season's mutability
Prevent us verdant hues to see.
And, after all, they still will stand
An emblem we can understand.

At Nantes, while lately wand'ring there,
And breathing balm from evening air,
Still westward strolling further on,
At last, surprised, I came upon
Grand rocks that yawn'd with quarries deep,
Round which the fair Loire seem'd to sweep
And change, still as it winding roll'd,
From distant blue to liquid gold.
A straggling suburb crowning heights,
The passing stranger then invites
To saunter on and thread his way,
'Twixt walls and figs, to Chantenay—
Bright, vineyard-smiling Chantenay!
Thyself so worthy of a lay.
A labyrinth of walls around,
O'er which bright trellised vines were bound,

Was intermingled here and there
With gates, which I was unaware
Admitted all who pass'd along,
Till I was told I did no wrong
In thus continuing my road,
While careless what way still I strode—
Through portals standing tall and fair,
As if some château had been there
In former times that could explain
Why such constructions did remain.
I fancied all around me show'd
Where once had stood some fair abode,
The glory of a former day,
Where dwelt the Sires de Luzançay,
A name which then I saw engraved
On these grim gates alone thus saved,
As if to tell to foe and friend   ·
Where feudal manners had their end.

But what surprised me more than all
Were rows of grand Magnolias tall,
An avenue prolonging there,
To make a northern stranger stare.
The shining leaves, so crisp and green,
Forming great spires with edges keen,
Show'd avenues on either side ;
The one commanded prospects wide,
O'er plains through which the bright Loire
    flows ;
The other iron gates did close ;

While now, except this avenue,
Nothing arrests the stranger's view
But small new tenements around,
Dividing the half-park-like ground.
To the sweet South I seem'd to be
Transported by that noble tree,
Whose strange tall branches ranged along
Might dictate an old minstrel's song,
Recalling days and men gone by,
For whom, at times, he well might sigh.

Deep silence all around me grown,
I wander'd up and down alone,
Surprised that walks so fair should be
Left as it were to secresy.
At last to try I was resolved
To have my doubts and fancies solved,
Suspecting that of this whole spot
The greatness was what now is not.
Then ask I needs must thus to know
If its true legend were not so.
To ask and hear should always be
Our part when meeting mystery;
For this cause surely it appears
That Nature gave us open ears,
Always open in old and young,
And not with lids like eyes and tongue,
In order that, both night and day,
We might just hear what people say;

And, hearing them, might thereby learn
What by ourselves we can't discern.
Now with wise books I must agree,
And think that women are for me
The teachers best when they are old
And ancient things have to be told.
These, sooth, are, like your pointer-dogs,
To mark out things in spite of fogs;
Rubrics they are of equity,
And full of grand antiquity;
From whom, at all times, admonitions
Will come the best for all conditions;
So salutary, prudent, wise,
That nothing with them ever vies.
For feminine old age abounds
In subtilties that know no bounds—
Holy and pure, yet Sibylline,
In which the past will often shine.
So then I would look round me well
To spy some old one fit to tell
The story of that ancient place
Where time I saw would all efface.
I had long while to seek and wait,
Till, seated at a way-side gate,
An aged crone at length I found
Who knew the legend of that ground.
She well remember'd where had stood
The château of the Seigneur good
Who own'd that fair and proud domain
Where beauty, grandeur, once did reign.

But when the Revolution burst,
There came a fierce, destructive thirst,
To bands who ravaged all around,
And levell'd castles to the ground.
The park, the gardens, courts and all,
Were sold in lots ; though they recall
The name of the possessor old
Whose goods were then dispersed and sold.

So thus I found what I had sought ;
The truth proved just what I had thought ;
And, as I said, the theme might be
Adapted to the minstrelsy
Of some poor wandering harper here,
To whom the past might still be dear.

I know, alas! his song would seem
To many like an idle dream.
" Fond poet," some would soon reply,
" What's past and gone in you we spy.
You trust in right, ideal truth ;
All that is obstinacy sooth.
To honour you would emigrate [2] ;
Such ways agree not with our state.
Our epoch needs an atmosphere
In which romance must disappear.

[2] From the French.

Men with their age must now agree,
And with their minute, as we see."

Undaunted still, our Bard would tell
What cannot please such critics well;
For though, like Piron, he may know
The courtly faults of Fontainebleau,
As when, from window's sly recess,
He saw each mask'd deceitful dress,
So mercilessly laying bare
The vanities that crowded there,—
Although he loves our low obscure,
He deems that rank should still endure;
Although these low have won his heart,
He needs must see the other part;
And he would have to sing of those
Whose turrets, vanes, and spires arose
Conspicuous over countries fair,
Denoting social greatness there;
Though, if the truth were sung of all,
Each then was but a noble Hall,
Where rich and poor did often meet,
In play and pastime simple, sweet,
To fleet the gay or serious hours
In hospitable, friendly bowers.
The high-born youth, in field, at board,
Was often by the poor adored,
Just as we see La Bourdonnay,
The Raoul with whom peasants play,

By equals and by peasants loved,
From upstart arrogance removed.
'Tis there, beneath the stately roof,
We find of Christian manners proof;
As, when we would trace pity great,
Inspiring those in highest state,
Our thoughts will often backwards flow
To ladies of the French château.
Nor need the Minstrel cherish fear,
As if no sympathy stood near.
He may invoke the statist wise,
Who French Reform call'd Social tries;
Who for our ancient ages feels
A fondness which he ne'er conceals,
Conceiving that between each class
True loving concord must surpass
Equality that now is shouted
Till social harmony is routed.
Le Play proves this existed most
Before the world had heard our boast[3].
And Grattan did the Bourbons praise
For much bespeaking Freedom's ways.
Your Minstrel too will touch the lyre,
Awaking notes that can inspire
Respect for that domestic life
With which new ways are oft at strife,
When in each ancient family
You saw the type of monarchy,

[3] Le Play, "La Réform Sociale en France."

A kingdom in itself alone,
Where each would simple duties own,
A union with one common bond,
To which each sought to correspond,
Regarding the heraldic tree
As proving he should knightly be,
In placid thoughts and maxims high,
Nobly to live and bravely die.
Nor would he yet forget to sing
Of servants, and the lowest thing.
Whom Athenæus little dreamt
Could be from ancient vice exempt.
Old Plautus, Terence, never knew
Such characters as here we view,
Familiar, faithful, just, and fond,
Attach'd still by the sweetest bond
To those whom they were proud to serve,
And from whose side they ne'er would
    swerve,
Their lives a theme for gravest pen
That show'd them types of honest men ;
So far from indicating taints,
Enroll'd were some among the saints,
Like Zita, humble, lowest maid,
And valets, who to masters paid
The debt of grateful constant love,
Till Heaven received them, crown'd, above.

So thus the Minstrel, lowly bow'd,
Would, smiling, play on to the crowd,

Half fearful lest his lowly song
Might seem beneath a noble throng ;
But then, as if still dreading eyes
That homely, simple themes despise,
He'd gently touch the sweetest wire
And sing what most will yet admire,
That friendship, as in old romance,
Which still exists in gallant France.
For there as realized you hear
Old Hesiod's proverb, quaint and clear,
That Friends who live too far to call,
Are not in fact true friends at all [4],—
A maxim foreign to our day,
When men to Business worship pay.
The Minstrel too would fain describe
What to these races all ascribe,—
Their constant care that no offence
Should rudely wound another's sense ;
Of which the counterpart we see
In Richard's want of courtesy,—
That English king's unfeeling taunt,
" How is it now with aged Gaunt,
Thou now a-dying ?"   coarse rough
    way—
Just like what some amongst us say.
Nor would he then omit to sing
And forward graciously to bring

[4] τηλοῦ φίλοι ναίοντες, οὐκ εἰσὶν φίλοι.
                                 Athen. lib. v.

That perfect elegance of mind
Which in these circles strangers find,—
That exquisite deep tact and taste
Which never yields to any haste,
To any passion, fear, or will;
Ever the same, and faultless still,
Amounting to a mystery,
So full of life and history,
The ancient and the new as well,
A true enchanter's potent spell,
A chronicle of knighthood past,
Each trait more charming than the last;
While over all a Christian tone
The schools themselves would not disown.
We hear now only of their crimes
From those who seek to guide our times.
Our Revolutions leave a breed
Which ancestors disdain to need.
Quite self-created, spirit all,
It says constructions old must fall;
Sooth, "pulverized, we hear, must be
All ancient aristocracy;
That, henceforth scatter'd to the winds,
Ideal things may rest in minds.
The future history is near,
Where total changes must appear,
Ad usum populi, they say,
Adapted for the present day.
As if the people could be brought
To entertain the sophist's thought!

As if they wish'd, like him, to see
Nought but foul deeds and misery !
This is what sophists overlook ;
They say, therefore, the future book
Of history about to rise,
The past no more will please our eyes ;
And study will be obligation
For men and boys of every nation.
Forbidding marriages the rules
Till each has means for future schools.
Magnificent remouldings then
Will form a race of knowing men,
Instructed to feel fiery hate
Against the former Christian state,
Its virtues not to understand,
Its faults alone to spy and brand."
To spy and brand all vice is well ;
But then the whole truth it should tell.
From crime these ages were not free ;
But crimeless races who will see ?
'Tis easy, sooth, to see their faults ;
Not always so to scan their thoughts.
" Reproachless " was an empty name
Which knightly hearts did most disclaim ;
Or else it meant a high appeal
From men who cannot depths reveal.
Blind to its faults, you ne'er could see
The graceful, grand old chivalry,
Which, even in decline and death,
Was humble to its latest breath ;

For when disdain man's blame it must,
To Heaven it own'd itself but dust.
It never knew the word "*correct*"
Implying it had no defect,
Like some who seem such models now,
Their worth consisting in a bow;
While each, to worst an enemy,
Is calculating secretly,
With manners that you might compare
To Winter chilling Friendship there[5].
But here were love and fervour strong,
Men never coolly in the wrong;
Wild children, who might mothers fright,
Not always doing what was right,
But never acting the profane,
Because they recognized their stain;
While, if occasion, let them show
True fondness, then their hearts you know.
They move thus often in a field
Where they can claim no human shield,
Aye open to much declamation
For the cool herd of every nation;
But, possibly with much to lack,
To angels they seem'd not so black
As to our zealots in their ire,
Who find there's nothing to admire,

[5] χειμὼν δ μειρακίσκος ἐστὶ τοῖς φίλοις.
Athen. lib. x.

If great hearts faults they think they see,
Yielding to them Sardonic glee.
For Heaven and women oft the same
Defects will like or load with shame.
Not merely mothers love to find
What's nearer to an humble mind
Than the black spirit now that soars,
And each proud adept loud adores.
I dare not sing, but you conceive
What here I must in silence leave.
Enough, we see here much to mourn,
But not to make seem quite forlorn
And void of Christian graces all
What we the *ancien Régime* call.
Man's weakness was not then denied,
But never was it shown with pride,
Defended as a trophy vast
Obtain'd o'er men and ages past.
As when the Tarentines of old [6]
Invited all eyes to behold
What vicious progress there could be,
Which each that liked might daily see;
While chiefly He look'd on their feast,
Of whom in truth they thought the least;
Who saw them, and directed thunder
With vengeance that made nations wonder.
No; such was not the weakness then
Of these light-hearted, gallant men;

[6] Athen. xii.

'Twas weakness, not that of the base,
In which no spark of good you trace,
But such as highest hearts may fear,
And o'er which saints will drop a tear.

Yes; there are names of chequer'd kind,
I need not lead them back to mind,
Like those whom Christ on earth absolved,
However men might be resolved,
Those too whom He redeem'd and chose
As His great human act did close—
Whose faults can make our choler rise,
To whom He promised Paradise.

Ah! well, this Minstrel's hand I see
An instant raised quite stealthily,
To dash away the lucid drop
Which threaten'd all his skill to stop.
So now with cheerful merry change
His fingers through the strings will range;
For he will sing of what will last
Harmonious with the noble past.
Yes; still, now, only look around,
He says, and much of this is found.
Since now, wherever Faith remains,
Essentials all the rest contains,
Be it the substance or but skin,
Thought, deed, mere polish, all's within.
Repair, for instance, to the fête
Parochial, dear to every state.

The Noble and the Peasant there
Have more in common than the air.
A frank familiarity
Binds close together each degree.
I sing not of the gay quaint scene
Such mediæval groups between,
Nor is it an artistic view
That I would now present to you;
Though, gather'd round the village cross,
Where rings for toys the children toss,
I know you could not but admire
What can simplicity inspire;
But, sooth, the beauty of the whole,
To drink which I would ask your soul,
Is that true, perfect freedom, ease,
Which makes the great desire to please
The simplest of that rustic throng,
As if to it he did belong.

But passing over things of pleasure,
Let thoughts now seek a higher measure,
Well suited to a lofty strain
Where nought is frivolous or vain.
So now the Minstrel, raising eyes,
And while his poor heart to Heaven flies,
Invites you, with expressive glance,
To think of old religious France,
And see her now brought back to view
By simply visiting the new.

While passing, then, to Luzançay,
He sings what stood upon your way—
That noble church which bears the name
Of Louis of such holy fame.
Oh! list to the unearthly sound
With which he waves you to that ground,
At the bright Sunday's vesper hour,
When radiance, like a brilliant shower
Of stars, descends from altars high
Amidst the loud Hosanna's cry.
Then come forth troops of maidens fair;
High noble dames will then be there;
The sturdy peasants pass along
In troops to hear the holy song—
The matrons holding children's hands,
The youths in fair decorous bands—
They hasten now from every side,
From all those quarters far and wide—
The noble from his mansion nigh,
The student from his garret high,
The merchant from his rich retreat,
The poor from fruit-stalls in the street;
The high, the low, the medium class,
All gather'd now in one full mass
To chant or hear Davidic Psalms,
And then, low kneeling, with join'd palms,
To hail the altar's mystery,
And Sacramental Presence see,
At that grand moment last, supreme,
Surpassing all the brightest dream,

When Benediction, as of yore,
Will leave no place for rapture more
In hearts that here alone can be
Taught Heaven's truths, veil'd mysteriously.

And lo! what beauty shed around!
What types, what passing shadows found!
When there in painting you descry,
The mystic glories of the sky,
While marble-white as angel's stole
Murillo's vision must control.
But see the kneeling crowds that there
Repeat the old familiar prayer
Which wafted generations past
To Heaven, where they will ever last;
And in each beaming kindled face,
Whose smiles bewitch'd you once, you trace
The dames and maidens holy, bright,
The sires and brothers, like the knight
Of earlier days, who just so knelt,
And just the same impressions felt.
Nay, further back through Time's dark night,
Great Pontiffs, heroes, burst to sight—
Donatien and Rogatien, Clair,
Apostle, patrons cherish'd there—
Eumelius, Felix, Friard, saints—
All those whom Fortunatus paints,
Seem there intoning still the prayer
Which round the same walls echoes there.

Then through the varied crowd at Mass
Duke Peter and his Duchess pass—
Frances d'Amboise, that "*Duchess Mother*"
Who lives, methinks, yet in another
That with her virtues still will deck
Nantes, which now sees Kersabiec.
As girl, wife, matron, duchess, saint,
From living models we might paint
That noble dame of ancient times,
Whose glory here shall grace my rhymes.
No strain'd conclusions these, to draw
From what exists and what I saw;
Since Nantes her children still has bred
To follow where her saints have led
The way, through Faith, to all the flowers
Which shed perfume on ancient bowers;
Through Revolutions, times, and tides,
The one old Faith there still abides [7].
Then, too, amidst these groups appear
Yet other manners living here.
Such as survived when many fell
Sad victims to seductive spell.
Still we detect the gracious train
Which deck'd the last illustrious reign
Of monarchs of the Gallic land
Who could yet docile hearts command.

[7] Siochan De Kersabiec, "Hist. de Françoise d'Amboise,"
Introd. xv.

Oh! manners of old noble times,
As musical as distant chimes,
Oh! gift of Heaven's benignity,
When their last traces we can see!
I care not if my verse offends
When saying that these grace my friends.
D'Esgrigny's cheerful, happy pair,
Who wearied, wounded hearts repair;
Gentle and gracious, constant, true—
Who make life wholesome thus for you.

So all those generations past,
In some now present, seem to last,—
In those who here around you kneel,
Who in the main the same truths feel,
While time all stealthily will glide,
Stealing in silence at your side,
Onwards, but with a baffled aim,
To see these Christians just the same
As those whom he had hoped to slay,
Now children of Eternal Day.
So thwarted thus in all his strife,
He here beholds the ancient life,
Its thoughts, its hopes, its wishes all,
Reigning supreme in great and small,
And thenceforth feels that all his might
Extends but to the smallest mite
Of that great social life below
Which from the Cross will radiance throw

Encircling in one bright embrace
In every age the human race,
Distinctions, raiment for a day,—
And nought besides to pass away.

The Minstrel oft has felt the calm
Which evening sheds with fragrant balm,
While autumn's myriad leaves will lie
On swoll'n brooks that murmur by,
In circles whirling, oft has seen
Their giddy dance gnarl'd trunks between,
And felt such revels somehow brought
Food for long musing wild and thought;
But ne'er to him were accents sent
More tender than these trees present—
As living tenants that recall
The manners of the ancient hall.
Effaced its turrets, gardens, wood,
Yet these poor files unshaken stood;
As if things springing from the field
Could thus for us examples yield
Of constancy and order too
When wild confusion visits you.
Some sympathy with plants, I own,
That Minstrel never could disown;
Things so benignant, beauteous, clear,
As friends of man must still appear;
And well he may esteem them so
When all their good deeds he will know,

Their purifying mission ever
Accomplishing with kind endeavour,
When, for his respiration, air
They still so skilfully prepare,
While yielding shelter, fruits, and shade,
And silent friends themselves are made.
The ancients thought that trees had souls ;
Such fancy mankind oft controls ;
But that they can prove friends I know,
To cheer and sweeten life below.
At least Magnolia's noble tree
Has taught and eke enchanted me,
As if with drops from Eden's dew,
That glitter'd with aërial hue ;
So, join'd with thoughts of highest birth,
Are even leaves that deck the earth.
Oh ! may its gracious peerless flower
Still lure us to a brighter bower,
Where 'tis not avenues we see,
But Heaven's own bright immensity,
A central glory ever trod,
Within, without that centre, God.

LE FOLGOËT.

FOR some days past, in gardens fair,
Wind-smitten leaves, methinks, all bear

Marks that, like letters, secrets tell,
Could they be all decipher'd well.
Spotted are those that round us soar ;
Perhaps, who knows? there may be lore
Contain'd, as some have thought, in each,
Which might some mystic lessons teach.
Well, Fancy is a truant child ;
I like her even when beguiled,
When thus o'er florets she will bend,
And think in each she sees a friend,
Reading in fibril quaint, light stain,
What can some gracious thoughts sustain ;
Not like a pagan with his creed,
Or as old Druids, that would read
On leaves as on a written book,
From which an alphabet they took ;
But just as thoughtful Christians, wise,
Who nothing natural despise,
Will in the least, most secret things,
Trace sometimes what the Poet sings—
A hint, a finger, to suggest
By signs or fancies what is best.

How tender episodes of old
Would fall from lips that legends told
In days of yore, when men had tears
For what now foolishness appears !
We all, of course, are far too wise
Poor, soft, light things like these to prize ;

T

Though some to fleeting leaves will sing
What once to hear would charm a king.

Folgoët woods, in Brittany,
Beheld a far-famed mystery,
Which caused the present church to stand
Just as you see it, strangely grand,
In such a wild deserted place,
Where art has only left this trace.

A certain child, then, born there,
To school with others would repair ;
Which, parenthetically, thus
Disposes of much learned fuss
Respecting want of education
Of yore for those of humble station.
This little boy of scanty wit,
Assiduous would daily sit,
And try indeed his very best
To be instructed like the rest.
But Nature, for some purpose wise,
Opposed him more the more he tries,—
And, for some reasons of her own,
Still will'd that much should not be known.
To all 'twas evident and clear
That clever he would ne'er appear ;
He had a heart, affection fond ;
But, sooth, not vastly much beyond ;
Yet it was strange how oft he tried,
As if he had with others vied,

Though far too gentle to pretend
To equal any dear-loved friend;
And friends were all whom he saw there,
To vie with whom he'd never dare;
For had he even power, still
He would have wanted all the will;
Though, sooth, as if by instinct led,
He needs must work his little head,
That he might always do what's right
In his dear Maker's gracious sight;
While want of talent threw, each day,
Humiliations in his way,
Which others might be blind to see,
While wounding him quite silently.
Yet 'twas impossible to know
Him, and not all the fonder grow,
While moved to look at him with eyes
Of love which utterance defies.

But say, is it not always so,
When Love will with some pity grow?
The clever, who can all surpass,
Will praises, prizes, soon amass;
Nothing escapes from their control;
They stalk on proudly to the goal;
Quite careless whom they would insult,
If only their success result.
But then your heart will close its door
Against them, and that all the more;

While the weak child, with timid hand,
That knocks there, always can command
An entrance to its deepest cell,
For ever cherish'd there to dwell;
Yes, sooth, for ever there to stay,
When medals, prizes, pass away,
As in a soft and shelter'd nest,
Esteem'd, ador'd, remember'd, blest.

Well, to return now to our boy,
Who never felt unchequer'd joy.
That Saloün was his name 'tis sung,
Or Solomon in Breton tongue;
As if 'twere wish'd that e'en his name
Should prove to him a cause for shame.
So thus to school he ever went,
Obedient, docile, gentle, sent
Without much hope that he would see
A time of great proficiency;
But though his efforts proved in vain,
There was one lesson did remain
Within his mind, to prompt a tongue
The sweetest that could grace the young.
For one thing he did learn right well;
And this is all we have to tell.
With blessed Mary in his heart,
He fear'd no scornful scholar's dart.
"Ave Maria," he would say
Untired, every night and day.

He knew but Love; Love was his whole,
His wit, his learning, and his soul.
In Mary he had found a mother,
When he was left without another.
To her by day he always flies,
To her by night with closing eyes,
To find perhaps in golden sleep
More than what others waking reap
When Reputation grants their vows,
And crowns of laurel deck their brows.

But time for all speeds on its wing,
Stern changes everywhere to bring,—
Changes alike for strong and weak,
Both for the proud and for the meek;
And so our poor and slighted boy
Must even lose his little joy.
What skills it sending him to school
Much longer, such a useless tool?
His weak faint hopes must pass away,
No more with scholars must he stray;
Though he had felt an honest pride
When seated meekly at their side.
Poor and abandon'd, lone he stood;
At last he wander'd to this wood;
And there he thought a hollow tree
For him might now a dwelling be,
There having for his sole support
The alms of those who might resort

In passing to the forest wild,
Where he would stay, this hapless child.

Yet for one pleasure he'd provide,
Which might attend where he'd abide ;
And therefore did he choose this tree,
That always near him there might be
The fountain-pool which still is found
Refreshing that entangled ground,
In which he could enjoy his swim,
And cherish thus one boyish whim—
A trait of nature, to attract
Some who would now observe the fact ;
For youth can not all joy unlearn,
Though men and circumstance prove stern.

So weeks, and months, and years stole on,
And all his other hopes were gone.
Contented, meek, remain'd he there,
And fed his heart on love and prayer.
But now the times were troubled ; strange,
Fierce arm'd bands through the woods would
        range.
For civil war did prowl around ;
No rest or peace on earth was found.
'Tis said, some soldiers passing by
Did find the boy, and loudly cry,
" Say now at once what flag you serve,
That we may know what you deserve.

For Blois or Montfort? quick reply,
Or at this instant thou shalt die!"
Saloün, who woes of sundry kind
Must through his life still ever find,
Uplifts his mild and placid face,
In which no signs of fear they trace,
And meekly, cheerfully, replies,
As if they should not feel surprise,
" For Blois or Montfort what care I?
Ave Maria is my cry.
Pursue your way with sword and spear;
But I serve holy Mary, dear."
Pursue their way they did with scorn,
And left the simple youth forlorn.

But nothing lasts in mortal life,
Not even what some covet, strife.
So Peace resumed her doubtful sway.
"But where's the simple boy?" some say.
No longer found within the wood;
Some now on this would think and brood,
While knowing he would often stray
To churches, where he loved to pray—
In youth, and to his latest breath,
Preparing so for life and death.
But still his ways were secret grown,
And the wide world was all his own.
So, thinking he had elsewhere fled,
No more of him they thought or said,

Until some wanderer found that he
Had died within the hollow tree.
Thence, carried on a lonely bier
O'er which some shed a stealthy tear,
They buried him in holy ground
Where now that stately church is found.
For shortly after, passing by
Where they had found his body lie,
A tall white lily raised its head,
As if in honour of the dead.
But what did most astonish them,
On each leaf traced, they thought, *A. M.*
Was writ, as if that lonely flower
Had grown up thus to grace the bower
Of one who, while he held that seat,
"*Ave Maria*" would repeat.
Believe this if you will, or not;
But they determin'd on the spot
That this great church should there be raised,
Where Christ's dear Mother once was praised
With such deep, constant, simple love
As angels feel in heaven above—
That thus for ever it should be
A monument of mystery,
To teach us that the humble mind,
Thus quiet, docile, constant, kind,
Above all else will one day tower,
Just as that wand-like, lovely flower—
Immortal, glorified, and blest,
When fade and vanish all the rest.

So now let Pride pass on and boast;
It has its own increasing host
To echo what it loudly cries
When men like these it so defies.
Its triumphs I would e'en invoke,
And add what will it more provoke.
For, sooth, of yore men pass'd beyond
What here is sung, becoming fond
Of idiots, mystic, helpless beings,
And still providing for their feelings,
While deeming that a soul oppress'd
Within that frame had still its nest;
Thinking they work'd with Heaven's sweet
     plan
To dignify the heart of man,—
That He who prizes most the heart,
Had left for them that gracious part—
To foster human misery
When shrouded most in mystery;
They even would pourtray in song
The weak protected by the strong,
And feel that God Himself they served
When these they cherish'd and preserved.
Such thoughts, of course, will Pride dis-
     trust,
And deem its feelings far more just;
To Pride our Solomon will seem
The phantom of a sickly dream.
But still, remaining there will be
Some few to love this mystery

Of tender and indulgent thought,
Which seems with Heaven's own fragrance
    fraught,
To make the heart of man expand,
And thoughts of God to understand,
Who, like a human Father, oft
May love the weak and tender, soft ;
The one least happy, favour'd here,
Yes, more than all best prized and dear.

To Him be praises from the heart,
Who did to men such thoughts impart
As still can penetrate a stone,
And make our feelings like their own.

ROME IN OCTOBER, 1867.

Rome had long watch'd with anguish vast
Those who, like waves, were rising fast
To swell, as in the ages past,
    Most strong and yet convulsively,

A low deep murmur in the air,
With lurid darts at times to scare,
That show'd a desolation bare,
    Awaken'd fears most piteously.

Aghast, the crowds now heard the thunder
Around the earth, above, and under;
The wisest fill'd with dread and wonder,
    Awaiting all confusedly.

For strange men, bold, of every realm,
Had vow'd that they would overwhelm
The Church's Pilot at her helm,
    And root out Christianity.

And " *Rome or death* " was now their cry,
All ancient truth they would deny,
And every art ingenious try,
    The times will'd it so steadily.

Invoking Revolution vast,
Resolved to blot out all the past,
Declaring that the die was cast,
    And they would triumph rapidly.

They deem'd their schemes complete, secure;
They would no longer Popes endure;
New Liberty would all things cure,
    While imprecating hideously.

The Priests with their chief friends must fly,
" *Down Superstition,* " is the cry;
The reign long promised, now so nigh,
    Prepares their dreadful revelry.

So subtilly their plans are laid,
They only need a sudden raid;
Their power never can be stay'd,
    Such mighty force has Novelty!

Political dissensions vast
Will consummate their ends at last;
They've nail'd their colours to the mast,
    Their plot contrived so masterly.

What great resistance can they fear?
Their friends, disguised as foes, are near,
Whose arts make danger disappear;
    They still work so ingeniously.

The Power they might sole mistrust
Aid all their "*facts accomplish'd*" must;
The world's eyes now are blind with dust;
    Since all was done so artfully.

The Christians, in confusion wrapt,
Feel cheated, swindled, and entrapp'd,
All bonds of faith and honour snapp'd,
    The whole is wrought so cunningly.

So now the tempest was to burst,
As when the pagans rose up first;
Await its fury no one durst,
    O'er Rome so gather'd dreadfully.

No human hope, however pale ;
No wisdom, justice, can avail ;
Mere force, nought else, must now prevail ;
    With power all defiantly.

In vain some eloquence would spend ;
You see all gone ; no trusty friend,
And Christendom about to end,
    So lours the dark futurity.

Alone the Pontiff on his throne
Remains unmoved with constant tone,
Invincible by patience grown,
    With solemn fearless majesty.

Amerced of aid—with treason nigh,
With outraged sense of Honour's cry,
Prepared with constancy to die,
    Still standing true heroically.

So now the secret legions all
To arms obey the cautious call,
Lest their sly friends they should appal,
    By doing aught imprudently.

One thing alone they had forgot—
Yes, one alone provided not,
To crown their universal plot ;
    Perhaps they deem'd it visionary.

They had not reckon'd upon truth
Still acting with its spell on youth ;
They never thought of that in sooth,
    And of its daring faithfully.

When lo ! from all the Christian lands,
Rush fearless and united bands,
Obeying their own hearts' commands,
    To save such weakness manfully.

Right gladly would the Muse proclaim
All those who went, and each by name ;
But they sought nobler ends than fame,
    Disdaining it internally.

Let others point out whom they will ;
Let Nature's Love be pardon'd still,
When, with more pride than lyric skill,
    A son I name right joyfully

Who thither took his stealthy way
When crutches he could fling away,
Resolved with no words more to say,
    But he must join them instantly.

Then pour'd from Rome's old crumbling wall
The brave, whom Fury can't appal
When shouting forth its fiery call
    To its red-shirted chivalry.

Then swoln, convulsive was the tide
Of waves conflicting far and wide,
Sulphureous bolts on every side,
    Flashing fast so frantically.

Then onwards still the Zouaves did pour;
The blood-red bands could stand no more;
They fled; while Rome stood as of yore,
    Calm, grave, and strong supernally.

Now what remains? Can no one say?
Enough; from shame removed our day,
Can true devoted homage pay,
    And, thanks to youth, triumphantly.

From low disgrace our race is freed
By French, Dutch, English, Irish deed,
Commingled with the martyr's seed,
    To live for ever gloriously.

The Future, be it shame or glory,
Will all be told in later story.
True, as in grandest annals hoary,
    So grave with solemn mystery.

High Heaven will still complete its plan,
Whose depths no mortal eyes will scan,
For saving docile, ransom'd man,
    And that, as now, eternally.

THE WAY-SIDE INN.

How leaves drift, dancing to the wind,
A little later we might find.
I wish we could prolong our stay
To mark their sad half-merry way,
Sliding and hopping, rolling on,
Flitting fast by you one by one.
Who no compassion feels when high
On topmost branch he can espy
One solitary leaf still there,
Resisting the inclement air,
The rest now fallen to their bed;
He sole survivor; all else dead?
Who will not feel, when storms arise,
A certain thoughtful, sad surprise,
To see the flocks of leaves that pass,
Tumbling and struggling on the grass?
Some hurried onwards to the pond;
Then others flying far beyond,
Leaving their gardens for the road,
Far scatter'd in the wildest mode,
Lifted and drifted up and down,
Until at last they reach the town,
So flocking even through the street,
As Kensington is oft their beat,

Filling the doorway of each shop,
Poor things, as if at inns they'd stop.
When all their fluttering dance is done,
The stern grim Winter will have won
Over the Autumn victory,
When only snow remains to see.

Now evening homeward leads back all,
Obedient to its placid call!
Boys to their mothers, ducks to sheds,
Swans to their osier island beds;
Rooks to the woods so dark within,
Travellers to their way-side inn.

Herodotus from Lydian air
Traces the first good hostels fair.
Polydore says that those who sported
Account for inns where joy resorted.
By way of prelude, all we know
Is that inns oft continued so;
Where those resolved to seek their ease
Discover'd many things to please.
Our pensive Shenston even thought
No safer harbour could be sought,
No warmer welcome we could win,
Than in some humble way-side inn.
Great Johnson said a hostel-chair,
With friends conversing freely there,
Was " of Felicity a throne "
Which sages might delight to own.

U

But, what is no less true and sweet,
All inns for pastime were thought meet.
The song of " Young Folk without Care [1],"
In the old French, seems native there—
When Clement Maro for refrain
Sings in that simple, merry strain,
" 'Tis ease that pleases noble hearts,
And what they truly love imparts."
Shakspeare and Dryden, Goldsmith, more
Than I can name in days of yore,
Seem on this one point all agreed—
At times, for peace, to inns to speed.
The " *Pine-apple*," and " *Siren*" too,
All these great wits, with Raleigh, knew.
Our Sterne at Moulins found it so,
And soon forgot Maria's woe [2].
A fragment from sweet Virgil's Muse [3]
Invites you still an inn to choose,
Where pastoral delights abound
Like those in his Bucolics found.
" Avaunt!" he cries, " to-morrow's care,
Haste now to live, since Death stands
        there,"
While pinching ears, as if to say,
" I come ; so quick, live while you may."

---

[1] Ballade des Enfants sans Soucy.

[2] " Adieu, Maria! poor, hapless damsel !   What an excellent inn at Moulins !"

[3] Catalecta.

At inns within the ancient land
Of Wales, a harper used to stand
To welcome guests with cheerful strain,
Perhaps that they might more remain.
Permit me, then, to strike these chords,
And choose a theme which still affords
Some mingled matter for the Muse—
Gay mirth, or terror, as you choose.
For by degrees from smallest things
The subject graver matters brings.
Attend then kindly to the first
Which on your ear abruptly burst.

I would I could our fathers paint—
Their customs with expressions quaint!
To cry, " Saint Julien's fair hotel,"
Was to proclaim that all was well.
Eustache Deschamps, a wife to praise,
Says, only to describe her ways,
And all perspicuous to tell,
" She keeps Saint Julien's own hotel."
Pierre Tasserye, a pilgrim old,
In a rhymed Monologue has told
How at " *The Red Hat* " he did find
Refreshment even for his mind—
" A lodging vast, a spacious court—
An earthly Paradise, that port."
Eustache Deschamps found inns in France
Like mansions that could him entrance.

A castle in the German land
Appear'd to him not half so grand
As a mere hostel with the French,
Though no deep moats did it entrench;
Which proves Don Quixote, on the whole,
Mistaking inns, not quite so droll;
And even now stand often there
Inns quite like châteaux, noble, fair.
The vast old inn at Abbeville,
Changed to a convent, proves this still.
In gardens bright, high-wall'd around,
The guests such peace and pastime found,
That I with some did mourn the day
When we must needs pursue our way.

How Froissart loved to ride along,
Might furnish matter for a song
Respecting hostels in his day,
Of which he oft had good to say.
No inn to which he ever came
On journeys he forgets to name.
Espagne de Lyon at his side,
He through the South of France did ride,
Now at " *The Angel*," Montpellier,
And then at Orthez to appear,
At Cassères on the Garonne;
And thence to Espagne he is gone.
" *The Cross*," " *The Beauteous Star*," and
    " *Moon*,"
Elicit hearty praises soon.

Sooth, to their honour be it told,
These inns deserved no mention cold;
Montaigne is somewhat of his kin
At old Saint-Pierre le Moutié's inn,
"A charming, truly sweet abode,
For those who thither ever rode,
Good cheer, good beds, good honest folk,
And nothing that could e'er provoke
A French, or yet an English guest,
Who at '*Saint Nicholas*' would rest."
Near Lavenelle, in Italy,
He likewise found much honest glee,
Where, standing in a lovely plain
(He wish'd he could be there again),
The nobles all the country round
Best pastime in that hostel found,
With such good cheer as famed Guillot
At Amiens could then bestow;
Such as in Paris with "*The Moor*"
To find each visitor was sure.
Spoleto's inn could quite surprise,—
Such rest! such pleasure for the eyes!
Tables spread out in trellised shade.
Sweet rural feasts could there be made.
When Ovid sings the age of gold,
He but describes what there is sold;
He tells of eggs, and cheese, and wine,
Of perfumed air which there did shine;
Parthenope's enchanted grove,
Where Virgil pensive loved to rove,

Could not have taught him more to tell
" How doing nothing pleased him well."

Yes ; sages, poets, would agree
In inns a harbour fair to see ;
They loved its peace, so void of care ;
For no intruding Pests came there ;
Though prices were not quite so low
As old Polybius did show,
When but three centimes for the day,
He says, a Roman had to pay.
Bright Genius, that would glory win,
Would find its study at an inn ;
Great poets loved that quiet seat,
When with the Muses they would treat ;
And Joachim du Bellay cites
A grave historian who there writes ;
" For what the common people say
To mark he often there would stray."
" Who can deny," he then exclaims,
" That this example many shames ?"
Such birds found there a sweet repast,
Whose songs have never been surpass'd.
When Rabelais' own house became
An inn which bore the Lamprey's name,
De Thou lodged there with Calignon,
Who both would celebrate Chinon
For having thus a hostel made
To please its former master's shade,
Composing verses which remain

In a fine tragic-comic strain;
As when they say that life demands
Some merry tribute at our hands;
The well-known owner, now a shade,
Is at the change contented made,
To find that youth can dance and play
When all his books are swept away—
Greek and Hebrew, with Latin—all
Yielding at sweet songster's call;
And, what is better, base ordure,
Which woman's ears cannot endure,
The garbage of a drunken sot,
The sole thing she will pardon not—
That foul and true Augean stable
Cleansed thus to hold an honest table;
His house paternal could not be
More pleased than by such charity.

Then, too, of hosts I needs must sing,
O'er whom the Muse might incense fling.
One of Great Homer's heroes kept
An inn where guests had often slept.
Axilos, slain by Diomede,
Provided thus for strangers' need;
For he upon the public way
Would take in all who wish'd to stay;
So true it is, in ancient days,
That hosts might shine in lofty lays.
Some even cultivated mind,
And were to poets ever kind,

Often best patrons of the Bard,
Yielding him up their hostel-yard ;
As Shakspeare found hosts in his day,
When his first dramas he would play
Before an audience ranged around
The galleries that there were found.
Southampton's Page, sent to an inn
To look for Shakspeare there within,
To be discovered by the face,
The noblest that he there could trace,
Brought Marlowe to the anxious Peer,
As him who grandest did appear ;
When his keen master made him see
In Shakspeare more humanity.
Then Mézeray had known a host
Of whose long friendship he would boast ;
As Molière, too, with all his troop,
To live with Bergerat would stoop.
The host e'en, or, at times, his son,
The fame of literature won,
As Rivarole and Aubery
Supplied examples men could see.
In England we can Prior cite,
That poet tender, grave, and light—
Whose uncle, when an humble host,
Would doubtless of his nephew boast,
Who at " *The Rummer* " tavern found
Such inspirations all around,
That thenceforth he would never rest
Till of its guests he proved the best.

The " Water Poet," Taylor, too,
I must indeed make known to you.
Famed for his songs, he kept an inn
Where gallant lords oft laugh'd within ;
For youth and friendship form a bliss
Which on the Thames we seldom miss.
These knew him on the Thames of old
A boatman, as the tale is told.
This loyal host has left a name
Deserving of immortal fame.
For when his poor king, First Charles, died,
Those murderers he all defied.
His former sign, that very day,
Was miss'd upon the public way ;
And, in its stead, a crown of leaves
All black and funeral he weaves,
Proud Cromwell and his band to shame,
" *The Mourning Cork* " became its name.
That was a loyal Englishman,
And boast of him all hostels can.

Then often hosts were men most bland,
In Christian times and Christian land.
Duguesclin, with companions ten,
Found thus a host the best of men.
For seeing none with spurs of gold,
And hearing that these all were sold
To bear expenses on their way,
He said not one of them should pay.

"Good horses ten," he said, "here stand,
These all are at your lord's command ;
Five hundred sheep I have, and swine,
Three hundred tuns of sweetest wine,
Fine sheets and furs for richest bed,
Bought when my wife and I did wed,
These and all other things I'd sell
Now rather than not treat him well,
The best of knights, so brave and mild !
He'd die to save a poor man's child."
Then to his "*Meisnie*" thus he said :
"Let meat be brought, and tables spread ;
Serve these good guests with greatest glee,
With all that God has given me."
Then said the knight, "'tis good and well,
Saint Julien led to this hotel."

I need not cite old Chaucer's host,
He who was once the Tabard's boast—
How he could understand the holy,
Distinct from abject melancholy,
And how he to the shrine would ride
With priests and knights who show'd no
          pride,
Their common object being fair,
Though some unworthy men were there.

Another host we likewise see
In the old tale of "Patties three,"

Who proved himself so pious, bold,
That his quaint action should be told.
He was a man most charitable,
Still helping all when he was able ;
The poor and strangers found him kind,
With a true, tender, piteous mind.
It chanced a ship was cast ashore,
In which a merchant had his store
Enclosed within a log of wood,
Which floated where his hostel stood.
" 'Tis good for burning," then he thought,
So instantly his hatchet sought ;
For firing he would split it well,
When at his feet the money fell.
So then what occupied his mind
Was how its owner he might find.
He would interrogate each guest ;
The sum with him, he had no rest ;
The silversmith had wander'd long
To whom the treasure did belong,
Till, come by chance to this good host,
Of all his losses he made boast.
The other thought he was the man ;
But still he would devise a plan
To see if God wish'd it might be
His, or all doled in charity.
He made three patties ; one with gold,
The others fill'd with bones and mould ;
He bade the merchant choose his own,
Who chose earth first, and then the bone.

The host from such a choice concluded
That ancient claims should be eluded;
The avaricious slave shall see
That wealth should yield to charity.
Then, in his presence, he did call
The blind, and lame, and poor, to all,
Of whom he gave the money vile
Which would the merchant's heart beguile.

When the young orphan was betray'd
Near Lannion, the hostel maid,
By ruffians, while she show'd the way
By night through which they had to stray,
From her kind master's hostel old,
As is in Breton legends told,
She spoke with so much holy pride
The murderers did her deride.
" That monks or clerks have taught you,
        child,
We gather from your answers mild;"
" Not they," she said, " have taught me
        this—
I learn'd it from my father's kiss;
Beneath his roof my thoughts were those
Which now can all your force oppose."
Dead she was found at break of day;
'Twas near Saint Joseph's Cross she lay;
Her lantern there stood by the rill;
Its tiny light was burning still.

The inn was called " *The Pelican*."
Her mistress, as the legend ran,
A mother's love on her would spend,
But such was her lamented end.
Cedrenus tells another tale,
How hosts wish'd justice to prevail;
For finding once a traveller slain,
With whom his dog did still remain,
The landlord gave him holy ground,
And cherish'd in his inn the hound.
It chanced the murderer, passing by,
Would in the self-same hostel lie;
When lo! the dog, that fawn'd on all,
Now flew, with fury to appal,
At the wild stranger, whom the host
Arrested, at his risk and cost,
Until his guilt was found to be
Quite proved when tried, and hang'd was he.

Then Huguet Taillant, at Auxerre,
Host of "*La Monnoye*," pray compare
With the old English landlord bold,
Of whom such tales are sung and told.
" This good and honourable man,"
(I cite Collerye as I can,)
" Caused Churchmen with him all to find
Reception generous and kind;
Wealthy or moneyless, the same
Respectful greeting when they came;

Old or young, and without pretence,
He loved them as a man of sense.
For all men he was complaisant;
Nor did he for mere profit pant;
No ballad sung without his voice
Joining would there be counted choice.
His prices, neither high nor low,
Charged by his varlets did not grow.
If noiseless merriment did rise,
He was content to close his eyes;
Since for a little love and glee
Without offending, what cared he?
But he is dead; to Jesus pray
At His sweet side that he may stay."

Falstaff's blithe host at Windsor thought
That duels never should be fought.
When quarrels rose, he laid his plan
That neither guest should meet his man.
Both politic and subtle, he
Puts soon an end to enmity,
And with a glass of sack or beer
Once more he makes them comrades dear;
So, of " *The Garter* " then mine host,
Of peace-making will gaily boast,
An incident from Shakspeare's pen,
Which paints an English landlord then.
In Sarnen at an inn I saw,
A host whose portrait I would draw.

"Come on, my lad," he said to me,
"And let us now gay anglers be.
'Tis Friday; so you must have fish;
With these two rods we'll find your dish."
At Coblentz, on a Saturday,
My host did equal homage pay
Unto the Church's discipline,
Which then prevail'd along the Rhine.
For strangers he had made provision;
But abstinence was his decision;
And, marking that I too abstain'd,
He loved me while I there remain'd;
Leading me oft to all his books,
With friendly, patriarchal looks,
Saying that he could Shakspeare read,
That on his thoughts he sought to feed;
That he loved studious, pious youth,
And, more than all his profit, Truth.

But let a hostess now be shown—
The portrait is Claude Mermet's own—
A hostess from her early youth,
He paints her as she was in truth,
Intending nothing strain'd or sly,
As if he worked with irony,
To which some now his words ascribe,
Whose thoughts so well denote their tribe.
"Discreet, content with profit small,
She had the suffrages of all.

A creature wise, as you might see,
Aye dress'd with such propriety,
She wore her own hair when grown grey ;
For Death's-head's locks she would not pay ;
As a true Christian, charitable,
Some poor should dine at her own table ;
The sick to succour she would fly,
And comfort those about to die.
If she wax'd not so wealthy here,
Rich up above she will appear."

The feudal lords, who own'd the land,
Had oft these hostels at command ;
And sometimes, as if each were host,
Of his own inn the lord would boast ;
Though this was an abuse they claim'd,
Unless they have been much defamed.
At times the esquire of a knight
Would keep an inn, and all seem'd right.
The Count of Orthez, in Navarre,
Saw no indignity or bar
When his own squire gave Froissart
The lodging that so cheer'd his heart.
At Malines Albert Durer slept
Where the good inn a painter kept.
" *The Golden Head* " then saw a crew
Of those who would the artist view.
Painters, sculptors him there would greet
With greatest honours, as was meet.

Some inns through charity were raised,
As when Saint Remy's Friend was praised,
Atolus, who built twelve hotels,
As his old mouldering tomb still tells.
That hostels pilgrims might receive,
Great laymen would their treasures leave.
Those who to Palestine would go,
Had such a friend in Boucicaud,
The Maréschal, who at Arles left
An inn for them, if there bereft
Of other harbourage; so nigh
A convent should their inn supply.

But now observe the house as well,
For here was much to paint and tell.
An ancient poet, Portuguese,
In hostels a resemblance sees
To churches; Gil Vicente must
Prove a grave witness we can trust,
When in an "*Auto*," to the crowd
Devout he could this urge aloud;
Had not the inns been holy there,
He would not venture to compare
Things as analogous by name,
Which, placed together, call'd for blame.
But, sooth, inns wore a certain air
Which might induce him thus to dare.
At Radicoffani I lay
Once on the great Saint Michael's day;
When Mass was said within the inn

For those who then were lodged within.
Thus hostels lonely on the way
Had chapels, where some priest would stray.
Who knows but " *The Damascus Road* "
Was sometimes found by those who rode ?

That signs at Rome were known of old,
Has recently been fully told.
The mediæval hosts would paint
For sign the image of a saint.
" *The Three Kings*," as at Noyon, show'd
That mystery to those who rode.
" *Cygne de la Croix*," by way of fun,
Presented thus a harmless pun.
Montaigne, when pleased with any inn,
His painted shield would leave within,
Or cause it to be hung on high
For sign to those who pass'd it by ;
As at Plombières, shown on wood,
And where long afterwards it stood,
Which cost him, as he says, a crown,
To please the hostess of that town,—
A custom which, in part, remains,
And many signs of inns explains ;
But it is most within, on walls,
That painting guests' attention calls
To holy scenes and doctrines true,
Which there were placed within men's view,
As is described by sage Monteil
In his completely graphic style.

A good inn never could dispense
With pictures full of mind and sense;
A Crucifixion with the thieves
Must there be found, each host conceives.
Saints, angels, even Noah's ark,
The travellers should all remark.
Ye who to inns will now repair
For saints or pictures little care.
But let me your attention call
To those who loved the storied wall,
When cardinals would condescend
To hostels works of art to send,
Describe with true artistic glee
What kind of paintings there should be.
Grave Paleotus deem'd it meet
On this especial theme to treat.
Great Albert Durer had a way
Of giving pictures hosts to pay.
At Brussels thus, and in the night,
He painted, and by candle-light,
Good Master Conrad and his wife,
A son too, all done to the life.
To servants he would give, for drink,
Some picture that could make them think.
Thus to a certain John he gave
A Christ who died mankind to save,
And this he painted upon brass;
Away, with such gifts, he could pass.
At Halliford our host was found
A man of noble heart and sound.

x 2

For having order'd on a day
Five beds and supper on our way,
And not returning there to sleep
(The bells of Ouzeley us did keep),
He would not hear of being paid,
Since at Old Windsor we had staid.
Our boat flew quickly back to town,
But still our debt I jotted down.
Two pictures then I sent the host,
Of which, perhaps, he still will boast.
Not only would he let us leave
With payment such ; I must receive,
Some three weeks later, eels and jack,
Which in the picture-case he'd pack.
Thinking it empty, I had there
A bitten finger me to scare.
Alive they all came from the way,
And in our fountain swam away.
Nor for instruction was this all
Supplied by the old hostel's wall.
Each room, for number, bore the name
(And for that use they felt no shame)
Of some great saint, which custom holy
Keen satirists did mock at wholly ;
As Artus Désiré would laugh,
That men in " *Paradise* " should quaff,
Pretending he could not endure
Associations ; though I'm sure
The folly lay in his own brain,
That of things harmless would complain.

An inn, in mediæval times,
Display'd on walls some holy rhymes;
For, sooth, men never then forgot
Saint Joseph's inn, the Saviour's grot.
From Bethlehem I needs must turn,
Although the name makes hearts to burn.
Since thus the oriental Khan
Shows how this theme can interest man,
Combining the supernal high
With things that we pass daily by.

But ancient inns might often fill
The hearts of men with holy will.
For thus upon the Appian way
Saint Paul at Tres Tabernæ lay;
Where the new Roman Christians came,
Attracted by his mighty fame,
To meet him at those hostels three,
As if ordained with mystery;
For later their first church did rise,
All pagan hostels to surprise,
Upon another hostel's site,
When Rome beheld that novel sight.
Her Emperor himself did say,
" Let these strange Christians have their
          way;
Better a house of prayer, I think,
Than one where men will only drink."
In the last persecution fell,
Of which the Christian annals tell,

An inn became the chosen place
Where martyrs left their sanguine trace.
The Patroness of Augsburg then
That transformation show'd to men ;
Saint Affre, with her servant-maids,
The shame of former sins evades,
Converted all within the spot
Where female virtue was forgot,
Thus yielding proof to wond'ring Greeks
Of what old Athenæus speaks,
That there is seen a goodness strange,
Surpassing constant virtue's range,
In women of this kind, when found
Once changed to manners pure and sound.
For he, like many, must have known
The secret things which Christians own.
But even in the thirteenth age,
We find such marvels on the page
Of great Ducange, who tells of one
That souls within an inn had won.
Guillonus in all inns would preach,
Where no one else had dared to teach.
Then Constantine's great mother, too,
Within an inn comes first to view.
Saint Helen's father was a host,
Of whom hotels should ever boast.
In Helenopolis she came
Into this world, and thence the name ;
For England vainly seeks to show
How York first saw that flower grow,

Orosius putting quite an end
To fictions, though our breath we spend,
He deeming it no shame or sin
That she saw light first at an inn.

But now, since night is drawing on,
To other scenes I must begone;
To sing dark horrors now I'm led,
To send you terrified to bed.
Our Harper, thus you find, is sly,
And can your secret feelings spy;
So men and scenes you see must lour,
To suit, he thinks, the present hour.
For well he knows you feel delight
To hear of dreadful things by night.
So now grim facts to hear prepare,
And then to sleep if you can dare.

Oh, yes! it cannot be denied,
This theme presents another side [*].
So draw in close and hear the rest;
To know the truth is always best.
Inns, hostels, have no age of gold,
If we go back to times of old.
Plato excludes from civil rights
Him who for lucre guests invites.

[*] Francisque—Michel and E. Fournier—Hist. des Hôtelleries, Cabarets, Courtilles, &c. 2 tom. Paris, 1858.

He had his reasons past all doubt,
If only we would hear him out.
The Pandokeia Greek was thought
A place where nothing good was taught;
And Plutarch says, that friends there made
Were never good men, just, or staid.
A veil, indeed, should here be thrown
O'er facts that we must faintly own.

Throughout the Eastern regions vast
In mind we should now hasten fast;
And, if no friends invite us there,
'Tis best to sleep in open air,
For never with the ancient Jews
To lodge in hostels we should choose.
The Hebrews may have had their inn;
They won't refuse to take you in;
But all is doubtful there, obscure,
And only mischief is quite sure.
Rabbis, Septuagints dispute,
Whose feuds do not our purpose suit.
Of Rahab's inn, at Jericho,
The better all the less we know.
Brave Samson in an inn once hid;
'Twas not the wisest thing he did.
At Gaza, sooth, we need not stop;
'Tis best to let the subject drop.
Old Egypt, Palestine, could yield
A roof and walls that just would shield;

But mules or asses always bore
Provisions of the traveller's store.
The Hebrew host or hostess then
Had secrets worthy of their den.
With Greeks and Romans 'twas the same;
No grave man to a hostel came.
Isocrates was known to say,
No slave would in a hostel stay
To take refreshment, so reviled
Were all who there could be beguiled;
And, in a speech, Hyperides
Did likewise public inns dispraise.
Whoever supp'd beneath that roof,
From public acts must keep aloof;
The Areopagus would not
Permit such ways to be forgot;
So no such person thenceforth dares
To mount those senatorial stairs.
All venal hospitality
Involved a queer morality.
Xerxes, 'gainst the Babylonians,
Pass'd a decree, told by historians,
To punish their revolt and strife,
Condemning them to pass their life
In hostels which should furnish drink,
That they to lowest depths might sink;
And so, enervated, might be
Enslaved by merely that decree.
'Tis Plutarch who records the tale—
A thing to think on over ale;

So well of old men could distinguish
Faults, yet their comforts not extinguish ;
Like the poor, wretched, drunken sots,
Who only can be drawn from pots
By swearing they will drink but tea,
And no cups other ever see.
Excess—opposed to Germans' way—
Of which French Rohan's Duke did say,
" Perpetual motion's only found
Where Germans goblets pass around."
At Rome men gambled at their inn,
One of the pastimes found within ;
Claudius, the Emperor, would play,
Even when carried on his way.
Our gambling, betting, sporting crew,
Supply us thus with nothing new.
But Roman inns, found here and there,
Scatter'd o'er wide Campagnas bare,
All isolated on the road,
Of robbers' friends the known abode,
Presented other dangers deep,
Awaiting all who there would sleep.
For not to sing of curious eyes,
Of watchful and imperial spies,
Who made the " *Mansion* " but a place
Where they could all their victims trace,
Telling to prætorian prefects
Things that perhaps each least expects ;
Though, without letters of " *evection*,"
No traveller had there reception,

There were found dangers still more great,
As ancient authors will relate.
Poor Titus in a hostel fell
A victim to Domitian's spell.
Aurelius, in another slain,
Proves what black crimes did hostels stain.
Severus, Emperor, betray'd
At Tres Tabernæ, where he stay'd,
Was murder'd in that fatal inn;
His rival would the Empire win.
Ceditiæ, on the Appian way,
Attracted no rich man to stay;
Patricians shunn'd these public inns,
So noted for their frequent sins;
But Cicero, who loved to buy
All pictures that had pleased his eye,
Could not afford, like them, to keep
His private inns where he could sleep.
In Macula he found a host
Of whom to Lepta he could boast.
But mostly these were only walls
With roofs, and nought but what appals.
Assassinations oft took place
Where victims died and left no trace.
Though Virgil found in Copa one
To whose inn he had often gone,
Whom he could celebrate in song,
And, unlike Horace, think no wrong.
But this was an exception rare—
Inns were but dens then everywhere.

At Rome were trap-doors, through which fell
Guests at some inns, with none to tell
How they were forced to work below
The ground as slaves, which none did know,
Until a soldier forced his way
Back upwards, and the whole did say
To Theodosius, who destroy'd
The mills where they had been employ'd
In making bread, ne'er to be free
Till death should end their slavery;
As Socrates Scolasticus
Transmits the fact thus down to us.
In later times, it is the bed
Which sinks below; no space for dread;
So suddenly the victim then
Is join'd to subterraneous men,
With whom must pass his future days
In coining, or more desperate ways.
So some who came to drink or stay
But for a night were swept away.

Suspected and sinistrous wight
Was he with whom guests pass'd the night.
When the proud Tarquin wish'd to slay
Ticonus, he knew plots to lay
Within an inn, where he could find
Fit instruments to suit his mind;
And in such hostels still were those
Who would no treachery disclose;

Just as in later times, in Spain,
The Governmental spies remain,
Still hovering round the hostels, where
Gitanos proffer piteous fare.
As Bodin in an inn was made
By soldiers prisoner while he stay'd.
When Richard Cœur de Lion fell
Beneath the angry German spell,
Within his inn he was betrayed;
Where, with some Templars, he had stayed.
Disguised, he sat beneath the grate;
And, better to conceal his state,
He turn'd the spit that served to roast;
But then, abandon'd by his host,
He raised a knife in self-defence,
Until by rude main force borne thence.

The hosts themselves were murderers too,
As Cicero can prove to you.
Witness the poor Arcadian's ghost,
Who to his friend denounced his host,
As having kill'd him in the night,
And carted him at dawn of light;
Or only mark how Cicero
As advocate could such things know,
Engaged where mere conjectures lead
To true conclusions with such speed;
Though Clodius, murder'd at an inn
By Milo's men, who rush'd within,

Cannot be cited, since that host
From harm could no exemption boast.

But now, what is by far more sad,
The Middle Ages were as bad,
I mean, of course, respecting inns,
The chosen haunts of special sins.
Herosvita, in Germany,
Unrolls a picture few should see
Of inns in that eleventh age,
Unsuited to a moral page.
" *The Siren*," in " The City Match,"
Might have shown well what there did hatch.
The "Courtois d'Arras" in the next
Age, too, presents a spotted text,
Where the true Prodigal, wild son,
In hostels has his strange course run.
Like certain swells that you may know,
Whose lives are regulated so.
Then, too, assassination sheer
In inns caused men to disappear.
Thus, in the fourteenth century,
We find this strange and grim decree ;
That when in inns a stranger died,
And hosts to yield his goods denied,
The triple of what they retain'd
Was due to those who then complain'd.
Thus men to hostels could be traced,
But further, footsteps were effaced.

Of them no tidings ever more.
Thus, much was as in times of yore.
When Foulques of Rheims, that prelate great,
From murderers' hands had met his fate,
'Twas from an inn the brigands came
To work that deed of blood and shame;
And to an inn his servants brought
His body, which they long had sought.
Your Minstrel might go on to sing
Of terrors that grim tales can bring,
As in Saint Gregory of Tours,
Which our attention still ensures—
To tell of coiners in the inn,
To other criminals akin,
As on the Loire, at Saint Bénoit,
" *The Savage Man* " so often saw,
A hostel which there still remains.
Then he might tell in other strains
Of Breton's Geoffrey, when dismounting
With hawk on fist from ducal hunting,
On his way back from Rome, which he,
As a true pilgrim, wish'd to see,—
How, when his hawk a hen had kill'd,
His hostess, furious and self-will'd,
Had slain him, flinging such a stone
As left him dead without a groan;
Or, still more wild, at Beaujoulys
What at an inn one night did see;
When comrades two of Rodriguo
To an old hostel there did go;

When, hated by the country round,
As all such soldiers then were found,
They both were seized, while sleeping there,
And carried from that grim repair
Into the forest, which was then
The slaughter-spot of those bad men,
Where, stripp'd of all, their bodies lay,
When some roved there at break of day.

King Richard, ere at Bosworth slain,
Within a hostel did remain,
Where stood his bed, as moved each night,
All carved in oak, with arms bedight;
Beneath which, in a drawer, was kept
His hoard of money while he slept.
One servant-maid the secret knew,
Which on her fell destruction drew.
For when the battle there was won,
A cruel deed within was done;
When those who seized the treasure slew
Her who alone its presence knew.
There she lay, weltering in her gore,
That nothing might be blabb'd there more.
The tale is full of woe and dread;
But I slept once upon that bed [5].

[5] It is at Beaumanoir, the seat of W. Herrick, Esq., in Leicestershire.

The drawer still shown, King Richard's shade
Seem'd hovering with the murder'd maid.

The sixteenth century, as well,
Had histories as grim to tell.
Of hosts suspicion was so strong
That sometimes they did suffer wrong—
As Cordier's wife, and Bellenger,
From sad experience could aver.
Nay, what will many more surprise,
With ancient time much later vies,
Presenting, in the " *Kochmer-beys*,"
Dark facts that show the selfsame ways.
From Holland to the Danube stream
Pass'd things more strange than any dream.
Uninterrupted dark repairs
Are laid at every stage, which scares
The wayfarer, who vaguely hears
What ground he has for deadly fears.
Hosts, magistrates, police as well,
Were all combined, with hideous spell,
Like the dark secret bands that now
Against the Church have made a vow.
The spell that bound them was for gain,
By having helpless travellers slain,
Whene'er they slept beneath their roof,
That there might be no means for proof
Against the murderous secret band,
Who all their " *brothers* " understand.

Then politicians here might tell,
What Revolutionists know well,
That in such houses met the crew
Who shunn'd the day and public view.
Paris can still point out the spot
Of one great dark and recent plot.
For when the Bourbons were expell'd
Conspirators their orgies held
Where I myself have mused alone,
Though its fell secrets were unknown
To me, who would have fled the roof
Which of such mysteries had proof.
But let us keep to common crimes,
That better suit these hostel rhymes.

The lady [6] who through Spain did ride
From France, its inns could not abide.
Near some she saw the robbers' cave;
The host was oft an arrant knave;
The Sierra of Saint Adrian
Shows thus an inn, within the span
Of vaulted rocks, where thieves did lie,
To pounce on strangers passing by.
Salvator Rosa would have been
In ecstasies to have this seen.
Her host at Burgos had a way
Ingenious to extract great pay.

[6] The Lady's Travels, &c.

Within a spacious chamber shown
With forty beds she chose her own.
When scarce asleep, the hostess came,
Knock'd at the door, her needs to name.
" Fresh guests had come ; great señors all,
Who must have beds within that hall."
These dons illustrious stood there,
All hired, the poor French dame to scare,
Mere knaves, who knew the custom well,
All neighbours' sons, who would not tell.
The lady then refused assent,
The dons, profoundly bowing, went
Down-stairs ; the hostess, looking cool,
Declared, " no dame should her befool ;
For empty beds she must be paid."
And so did end this midnight raid ;
The lady robb'd as in a wood,
Though all by rule as understood ;
Low bows and scrapes instead of blows
The only difference that shows.

I a poor Minstrel once did sleep
Where snow for three days me did keep
In August, on the Alpine top
Of Grimsel, where still travellers stop,
Within a hostel lonely, where,
Since then, a host did foully dare
To murder his poor sleeping guest,
Who so did find a sanguine rest.

Y 2

In Sussex, having walk'd all day,
We reach'd a hostel on the way,
Just as the evening did decline,
And its last beams on Heathfield shine.
Low, solitary, small, it stood
For miles embosom'd in the wood.
Pedestrians have no choice left
When of all strength they feel bereft ;
So there perforce we had to stay—
We—for a friend had led the way,
Intending to have reach'd the park
Of Darby, knight of ancient mark ;
But darkness then fell fast around,
We shrank from six more miles of ground ;
So, wearied, and soon fast asleep,
We nestled until day should peep.
But oh! my friends, we little knew
What there was shortly to ensue.
At midnight woke up by a din
Of some who threaten'd, swore within.
I heard them mount, with oaths and vaunts,
That none should spy their special haunts.
My door was soon burst open, when
I saw a band of arm'd rough men,
Who, when they saw me raise my head,
Laugh'd, and with soften'd voices said,
" Psha! sleep on, lad, and never fear ;
We thought some other birds were here."
For this was an old smugglers' inn,
And they thought spies were then within ;

With whom accounts they would have settled
So furiously did they seem nettled.
You think, perhaps, I make too much
Of mean adventures, miscall'd such;
But be assured our lanes so green
Have midnight murders often seen;
And had this happen'd but in Spain,
I should not hear you now complain.
Well, to conform to your taste,
From English inns I now must haste;
Though I presume you'll let me tell
What to an Englishman befel;
For Englishmen averse to antic,
Must sometimes pass through scenes romantic.
Then, later still, this tale is told,
That well may scare the free and bold.
A Cambridge student pass'd along,
Thinking and fearing nothing wrong.
The South of France was then the scene
Where this wild fact did intervene.
Not distant was the arrowy Rhone;
A valley there had heard the moan
Of many victims in the night,
When all was hid from other's sight.
A solitary hostel there
He found, to which he would repair
At even, when the sun went down,
And he was far from any town.
The host stood, smiling, at the door,
And our poor student did implore

To rest his wearied limbs within ;
For farther he would find no inn.
But somewhat in that landlord's look
His nerves and resolution shook.
No ; there, forsooth, he would not stay ;
So pass'd, unharmèd, on his way.
But when a few short weeks had pass'd,
The secrets grim were known at last ;
For when some more had disappear'd
In that lone inn, it then was fear'd
That there had been and was foul wrong ;
When Justice rose up keen and strong.
The murder'd victims then were found
All cover'd near beneath the ground.
That host was hang'd, with all his men ;
And so was closed that fatal den.

Suburban inns, that stood quite near
To Paris, yielded equal fear.
In them Cartouche was often known
To hide, with others or alone.
In the " *Haute Borne*," at Courtille,
The archers had at last their will ;
Six loaded pistols by him kept,
They pounced upon him while he slept.
Then sometimes, when the hosts were just,
Their sons were not quite men to trust.
At Belleville, thus, a landlord's son
Had often robb'd and purses won,

Till travellers, at his father's inn
Seeing him seated there within,
Although the place was far away
From that where they did lately stray,
Did recognize him as the man
From whom, when robb'd, they frighten'd
   ran.
Dark Bondy's Forest all would fear,
But deeds as fell were practised near;
For cut-throat gorges could be found
On public roads with houses round.
And well I do remember me
Of passing, with companions three,
Across Saint Denis' plain by night,
And of our deadly youthful fright;
For these French lads assured me then
We walked by hostels, haunts of men
Who might, without the smallest fuss,
Start out and murder boys like us.
'Twas in the reign of Louis Philippe,
When lives by night cost not a fillip.
Perhaps you think this must suffice
To finish terrors in a trice.
But wait a little longer, friend;
To what is coming pray attend.

The wind in gusts begins to rise;
Each latch and bolt some goblin tries.
Hark! what a wild, protracted groan,
Of way-side groves the distant moan!

There's creeping down the chimneys high ;
Somewhere without there is a sigh ;
There's tapping at the window-pane ;
I would not now alone remain.
Strange noises, too, I hear below ;
That even I half nervous grow.
My harp must give accordant sound,
Like midnight howls o'er blasted ground ;
For, going back to Rome again,
You needs must hear a fearful strain.
The pagan hosts were thought to be
Oft adepts in black sorcery.
'Tis Saint Augustine who reveals
The magic spell that hither steals.
The superstition then was strong
Which deem'd that, to all other wrong,
The host would add a fearful way
To metamorphose guests who stay,
And dare not always keep aloof
From food prepared beneath that roof.
'Twas cheese, by magic rite prepared,
By means of which they still worse fared.
Then just in Apuleius look ;
I must refer you to his book—
(The first), in which, I think, you'll find
Some food for a romantic mind ;
But still tradition has its tales,
Which all through Europe yet prevails,
To prove that hosts, like shepherds old,
Were sorcerers both skill'd and bold.

The doctrinal De Sapience
Had never banish'd it quite hence.
The lonely, grim, and dreaded inn,
Was thought deep versed in magic's sin.
At Osenberg, grave Winkelmann
Found there a hundred-years'-old man,
His host, who said his father knew
Some facts that proved this might be true.
Gnomes from the mountains would appear,
With unknown money buying beer;
His grandfather would all this tell,
For he to spirits beer did sell.

That hostesses in Germany
Used magic, many did agree;
Bad spirits of all kinds 'twas found
In hostels often did abound.
Peter of Amiens would swear
That all pass'd as I tell you there.
A lonely inn, "*L'Eau Luissante*" named,
For strange appearances was famed
Of fairies; it stood near the well
Where those wild beings loved to dwell;
That hostel, so call'd, was in Hesse,
And near the castle there call'd Plesse.
In Spain, Quebara's Castle stands
Close to the inn which it commands.
That castle, haunted by its sprite,
Would frighten hostel guests by night;

The host its keys kept in his inn;
Few guests could close an eye within.

But soft! I see you now half dead
With fear; but go not so to bed.
Tush, child, sleep well, with tight-shut eyes;
For your poor Harper only tries
Just to inflict that pleasing fright
Which casts a wild tone on the night;
So now he strikes a lively air,
To smoothe down all your standing hair.

Rejoice, my friends, you now can speed
To stately inns from terror freed,
With grounded hopes that there you'll find
Rest, peace, refreshment, manners kind.
That there will be a fit supply
The ancient rules to verify,
That scholars breakfast, lawyers dine,
Merchants sup, where all is fine [7].
Then should you scorn such feasts, like me,
We've what will suit you to a tee.
Come to our way-side, lonely spots,
Small inns, like anglers', shepherds' grots,
With tiny gardens, all retired,
Where Nature's beauty is admired,

---

[7] Desjeusner d'escholiers, disner d'advocats, souper de marchands.

Known well to you, but hid away,
Where with a loving friend you stray,
By river's banks in fragrant bowers,
Where neither bill nor landlord lowers;
Where, though things are not grand within,
Between your teeth no spiders spin
Their webs, unless, like Thelemites,
You choose to live on sounds and sights—
Yes, come to our sweet homely shed,
Where nothing proud or false is said;
Where language is all simple, free,
Such as with Montaigne did agree—
Replying that, "all said and done,
I'd rather now have taught my son
In way-side hostels how to speak,
Than, in these schools of talk, to seek
That jargon of the pedant's class
Which taints what has through it to pass.
So speed to where, above all height
Of grandeur, is to say what's right;
Where youth can pass a happy day,
And, with responding eyes, still play,
Entranced in a Midsummer dream,
With tea, and bread, and fruits, and cream,
While reaping from some English heart
The joy which Love can still impart.
Bright Teddington and Halliford
Can such sweet pleasures still afford;
Old Kingston's "*Sun*" and Ditton's "*Swan*"—
How often thither am I gone!

The " *Spaniards*," on sweet Hampstead's Hill,
The same great purpose can fulfil ;
The " *Royal*" inn, at Beulah's Spa,
Suggests conclusions deep to draw ;
For royal truly all is there,
With which king's joys cannot compare,
When setting beams will fire the sky,
And on the sloping grass you lie,
No courtly pleasures there to be,
But two fond hearts that will agree.

Suburban inns with us are not
Dens such as France has not forgot.
Sevigné's gentle, simple shade,
Would not be here indignant made ;
As when near Nantes she found such fare
As her frugality could scare.
No more Erasmus now would sigh
To enter inns the way-side by,
Cosmopolite, like some of us,
At each inn making such a fuss,
Of something eager to complain,
With lamentations tedious, vain.
In fact, he found all inns so bad,
The thought of journeys made him sad ;
So, though invited by the Pope,
Great Adrian, to Rome, he'd mope
At home, through hatred of the stove
Of German inns, if he should rove.

But we, who wild adventures like,
From work like this need never strike.
Besides, an inn can still recall
High scenes, romantic, great and small;
Methinks the names of guests alone
Will often yield a lofty tone,
Higher than those in Phrygia old,
Of whose great records we are told.
The royal inns in Persian land,
Stathmoi Basilicoi, were grand;
Great Alexander stopp'd at one
When first against Darius gone.
Then Mithridates later came,
Attracted by the great king's name;
The lists of guests here still are known
Who hostels once had made their own.
And if the hosts who still remain
Are not precisely of the train
Of those we sung of, holy, just,
They've honesty which we can trust.
As when Montclar to Dessein gave
A sum he would from dangers save,
When passing to the English land,
Famed for many a robbers' band,
Receiving it on his return,
When he did feel his bosom burn,
That the good host declined receiving
A due receipt when he was leaving.
" 'Tis not my custom, sir," said he;
" You trusted in my honesty;

And now I trust in yours as well;
Besides, the register can tell."
With us such hosts, I think, abound,
As thus in Calais could be found.
If poor folk they do not receive,
The rich guests they will not deceive;
Their alms besides are often great,
Though not just given at their gate;
They have a mode that's quite as sure;
They leave for sisters of the poor;
To better times they keep that link;
So may no other virtues sink!

But list, one final touch, and we
Conclude our hostel minstrelsy.

Grave Diodorus tells us then
A custom of th' Egyptian men,
Remarking, that these people all
Esteem their present things as small,
Compared with what the future yields,
When Fame them from oblivion shields.
Therefore on tombs, he says, their kings
Employ their richest, greatest things,
While palaces they all disdain,
As places where they can't remain.
So houses for the living all
Mere inns and hostels they will call;
Whence they will quickly pass away;
Where no one is allow'd to stay.

Proclaim we, then, to one and all
Who sleep to-night within our hall,
That this should be their thought as well,
Whene'er they pull the hostel-bell,
Quite careless of what here they find,
Provided all be fair and kind,
Esteeming not an inn their home,
But home an inn from which they roam.
Disdain, oh! guest, to count the pelf,
As if it much concern'd thyself,—
The furniture of vessels piles—
At which a stranger only smiles.
Be not like Pytheas of old,
Who on his tomb would have it told
That in his life (his inn) he then
Had far more plate than other men [7]
Do order and enjoy while here
Such common things as may be near—
The blazing hearth, the comforts round,
Which in an inn may yet be found;
At pictures you may take a glance,
But nothing here should you entrance.
You should not heed what there may be,
Provided all necessity
Be here relieved from first to last,
Till from this *Mansion* [8] you have pass'd.

[7] Athen. lib. xi.
[8] The name for the old imperial inns of Italy.

Nay, more than this; I'd have you here
Deliver'd from all future fear;
That so a hostel may have taught
What others learn by deepest thought.
For look you—houses will remain,
Whatever sounds in moral strain;
At least for children, you may love
When forced from them you must remove;
But not so, that still fairer Pile,
In which you pass your life the while.
That structure of the flesh and frame
Which a true hostel you should name,
Will, like a ruin'd inn, be closed,
When you have briefly there reposed;
Silent and shut up it will be,
Abandon'd, to a mystery;
Deserted all, its owner fled,
Itself a spectacle of dread;
The shutters up, and all nail'd down,
Although it once display'd a crown,
Perhaps a giant for its sign,
Or else an angel fair, divine.

Then, friendly guests, companions fond,
Oh! look this poor brief life beyond.
Apollo's precept be thy care,
" To know thyself"—a lodger there;
For Cicero does thus explain
The meaning of that Pythian strain.

To " know thyself" upon the whole
Is but to know thou art a soul,
Stopp'd at a hostel as you roam,
Till you can reach your future home.
Spend not so much upon this inn,
Where for a night you're lodged within.
Guests gain so little from its show!
From all the pomps it can bestow!
Sooth, great souls in their inn would hate,
Like noble guests, affected state.
Disdain to think your inn can be
Made suited to your dignity,
By nonsense such as apes command
Whene'er they would invent the grand.
No; let your favour'd inn be found
Where ease with nature will abound.
For Nature did contrive it well
As we must own if truth we tell.
By symbols consecrated all,
Like other inns that saints recall,
It seem'd to promise to its guest
A placid, sweet, and holy rest.
Alas! that it should prove my lot,
As if all this were soon forgot,
To sing of what may yet ensue
To me, and most of us, and you,
When all its dangers we have known,
And wish'd that we could them disown!
A moment more, and this must be
Confess'd with perspicuity.

At present I would only praise
Its homely, honest, harmless ways.
It wants no beauty from our aid,
By a true Master's hand all made.
It has provision for us all,
What's sought by guests, within their call—
Its reading-room for Wisdom there,
Its hall for spreading varied fare.
Contrivances to meet all wants,
And then its purely pleasant haunts—
Its slopes, and groves, and merry maze,
For those amused by simple ways.
Pass to its garden, laugh, have fun;
In gambols join that there are done;
Its pleasures are unlike the store
At home, where you will have much more
All free and safe, and no doubt pure,
With youth for ever to endure.
But then at inns we needs must see
What with our home would not agree;
So travellers have compensation
For woes inherent in their station;
And it would be but madness pure
To think what's coarse in inns to cure,
Forgetting that what's elsewhere had
Would here be out of place, or bad.
Take then thine ease within thine inn,
Remembering who is lodged within.
Enjoy all in an honest measure;
'Twas built, indeed, to yield you pleasure;

From its eyed keep, which all commands,
To the arch'd base on which it stands.
Rejoice in each wise comely part,
So clearly wrought by the great art
Of Him who, treading on our ground,
Forgiving and humane was found.
It is your inn, prepared, design'd,
To please a bright and humble mind;
But think not home it e'er can be,
Where you can all you wish for see.
Alas! I need not you remind
How small are its attractions kind!
How utterly inadequate
To satisfy your present state.
You scorn what even you possess,
With loathing words cannot express.
The things in one sense truly yours,
I wonder if your mind endures?
Old sketches, paintings—yours they call;
But on your fancy how they pall!
How satiated you will feel
With works that by-gone things reveal!
Sooth, much you inwardly will spurn;
Though where in that inn can you turn
And not find each thing used and stale,
Recalling but a weary tale?
And then, what's yours but for the day,
Must be an empty, fond display.
To like it, even were you bent,
You know it is not yours, but lent.

The sole thing there that does not tire
Is mankind in its true attire.
And why?   Because in them you trace
The air of a celestial place.
Yes; in your inn with you will stay
Those from whose side you ne'er would stray.
But mark, those hearts and faces fair
With you will never tarry there.
They stop a night; then, one by one,
They hurry off, till all are gone.
So courage! raise aloft your mind;
And wish not to be left behind.
Sooth, take your ease, as if by night,
Within your inn; but with the light
That dawns for an Eternal Day,
Oh! wing'd with love, pursue your way.
Howe'er you hope to find your ease
In such an inn, nought long will please.
But then, why stands it in this place?
Only to shelter for a space.
With such precision 'tis contrived,
That this space should not be survived;
For if you will prolong your stay,
Instead of pressing on your way,
The things which there to keep you thought,
Become such as you never sought.
Oh, wondrous skill! all art surpass'd!
Just while you want them things here last;
And then proclaim that you should leave,
Unless you will yourself deceive.

Nay, even when arrived at first,
You cannot wholly quench your thirst.
This inn seems truly often bare.
When even youth will it compare
With that bright home beyond the skies
To which, at times, its fancy flies.
The best thing, sooth, in every one,
Is the long list of those now gone,
Who, like you, lodged there for a day,
Then left their names and pass'd away.

Then mark now the world, how 'tis whirl'd!
You see the flag that's oft unfurl'd.
And e'en in you—how shall I dare
To sing of what perhaps is there,
By circumstances if beset,
Entangled in your hostel's net?
For what romantic tongues will tell,
In real life is found as well;
Perhaps what they bring forth to view
Might all be found consuming you.
That inns had snares of old you know,
With fatal traps since long ago;
So here, against your will, you found
Fresh nets that caught you all around.
But who could sketch or fancy all
The curious webs that may enthrall
You who would have scorn'd to be
Not fair and open, constant, free?

Some demon surely haunts each inn,
Malignant, working there within,
With difficulties to perplex,
Impossibilities to vex
Those who of Providence complain ;
Though He it is who would restrain
That foe so cruel to our life,
The real cause of all its strife.
This phantom grim, this enemy,
Makes you even falsely see—
'Tis he who makes you doubt your
    friend,
That to some other you may wend ;
Long absence, silence, mystery,
Deceive you ; but, in sooth, 'tis he
Who causes all things to go wrong,
Till broken hopes you drag along
In one sad chain that coils around,
Till you sink, fainting, to the ground.
And even were it otherwise,
The inn itself will oft surprise,
It has such steps, such strange turns dark ;
Let us but only one remark ;
Take ties brought back you thought were
    gone
For ever ; two, instead of one,
Then binding you with equal force,
Of complications strange a source,
Like those of the crusader old,
As in the tale so famed of old,

Since even Honour seems to say,
Now snap not either quite away.
Would it not fit a tragic song
When what you do must needs be wrong?
Though Love and Honour both agree
No other course was left for thee,
So marvellously wove the chain
In which, perforce, you will remain!
The knots, too hard to be untied
By you, contented to abide
To see if time some succour brings,
Untangling what around you clings.
Once never dreaming such a fate
Could so confuse your mortal state,
Hating what's evil more than blame,
Yet now in toils without a name;
Sunk by degrees, while never thinking
That through such pits you could be sinking--
You who but loved the wholesome air;
And now, behold, 'tis you are there!
Yes! incidents quite unforeseen
Here metamorphose men, I ween.
The very type they love the best,
On which their fancy sole can rest,
Comes to be placed beyond their reach,
With nought but sorrow there to teach,
Their one sole solace 'midst their lot
Being but this, " *they meant it not.*"
In tales you have this fate reveal'd,
While each is in his inn conceal'd.

Oh! what a wounded name may last
When from this inn each will have pass'd,
With no one left to stay behind,
Its webs entangled to unwind;
To know how it did all produce,
Perhaps thus yielding some excuse—
To mark not things with indignation,
But deem there is extenuation,
When view'd not in bold, hard relief,
But soften'd down, and grant reprieve,
Like that which even Wordsworth thought
Might be for him who humbly sought.
Conventional, material things,
So load and clog our spirit's wings,
That each can obstacles create
As insurmountable as fate,
At least for some too soft and tender,
Who for their faults can't reasons render.
Men will denounce, condemn, deny,
But God may hear the secret sigh.
So since such consciences may see
From blame they can be *elsewhere* free,
When weigh'd in that crystalline scale
Where touches from the Cross avail
To make it sink, while what will seem
Man's solid worth would kick the beam,
'Tis surely not so sad to leave,
No more Hope's chaplets here to weave
Where they will wither, and betray
Each guest who has no other stay.

You see you must not trust the inn;
You know not half the bad within;
Of all such inns run strange reports;
Each has his tale who there resorts;
But this is evident to view,
'Tis an odd inn, yes, old or new.
Both men and women, many, sooth,
Of its dark secrets know the truth.
'Tis only safe for guests most wise,
Who can't be taken by surprise.
I'd have you think there's danger nigh
Unheard by ear, unseen by eye.
The inn will have its way I know;
It always was and still is so.
Trust now your old experienced Bard—
While lodged there, stand upon your guard.
Yes; dread it, rather than the day
When, with hope safe, you pass away.
And, pray, what is it at the best,
When it has yielded fev'rish rest?
You have not seen its phantom yet?
But how much there you would forget!
Then, too, this wild, polemic din,
Is only uproar of the inn.
For look on what it represents;
The common inn all this presents.
You find in hostels of each nation
The story of the Reformation,
A protest of the stomach first,
Before the mind pretended thirst.

From inns, in thought, you cannot sever
The German doctor's bold endeavour.
Geneva's famous legislator,
Of France the ruthless Devastator,
In this was likewise of his kin,
That his first act was in an inn.
From " *The Four Nations* " to " *The Bear* "
This silly turmoil all is there.
In " *The Black Bear*," at Orlemonde,
Another chief defied and groaned ;
While Noyon's landlord's son might dare
Sow any discord while good fare
He gave on Fridays, Vigils, Lents,
Inviting all to Israel's tents.
In hostels thus the fearful word
" Religious hatred " first was heard,
Which young and old set by the ears,
And make us all shed secret tears.
And so, too, half your present wrongs
To this symbolic inn belongs.
It is this inn of flesh and bones
Which causes all these midnight moans.
For were each guest deliver'd free,
Dissensions he would never see.
But while he gropes beneath that roof,
From ill he scarce can keep aloof ;
For, most of all, these vain pretexts,
These calumnies of rival sects,
Mistakes, suspicions, jealousies,
Are oft but this inn's mysteries ;

Though e'en some guests, I grant, will bring
Fresh virus for the odious thing.
And then, for them, what Plato said
Were better for their heart and head,
That they, unto their inn affix'd,
Should only have its ways unmix'd;
That to it, fasten'd by a nail,
No vice of spirit should prevail,—
Since, when compared with such a guest,
The foulest common inn is best.
But wheresoever be the fault,
It still within this inn is brought.
So controversies sadden life;
The proud dark guest foments the strife;
Then friends fall off, or frigid grow,
Since their opinion wills it so;
However little you affect
To court the censure of their sect.
But it is idle to deplore
What will continue as of yore.
In brief, while here, howe'er you strive,
Ten thousand evils must survive;
For, whatsoever be the ill,
Its scene is in this hostel still,
Whether itself should cause the fault,
Or by its guest the whole be brought;
So in that sense it needs must be
The cause of all your misery,—
Yes; crimes, dissensions, hostile thoughts,
Perplexities, disorders, faults,

Whatever be the special woe
That round about you springs to grow,—
The complicated, heavy bond,
Which makes your feeble heart despond,—
The inn, the inn, the inn's to blame
For all this complicated shame,
While yet the more you wish to stay,
The longer bill you'll have to pay.
Why seek to dally and remain?
'Tis all the same old work again.
The room precise in which the mind
Has rested, no one yet can find,
So dark, mysterious is this inn,
So little know we what's within.
But wheresoever be the cell,
It is not home where love should dwell.
A vaulted puddle night and day
Should hardly tempt there long to stay
A guest so noble and so free,
Who loves a glorious liberty.
Sweeter to part, fly any where,
Than stop in such a hostel there;
At least you'll find all other good,
When thus your own is understood—
Your inn, which still your spirit soils,
So dangerous—so choked with toils.
One good at least may here be had,
You'll never call another bad.

Nor even now is this the whole
Of what should wing your parting soul.
For there how soon are men forgot!
Ay, just as if they had been not!
They thought mementos some would
    prize,
Themselves brought back to loving eyes—
Ah, me! no sooner are they gone,
Than all are swept off one by one.
Mark, too, what worthies will remain;
I do not want you to complain.
But many you must see whose ways
With judgment cool you cannot praise.
You need not cry "I'm sick of men,"
But, with Aurelius, think it then.
Let cynics shout out, make a boast,
Do you to silent thoughts trust most.
Poor Cicero, with later breath,
Said he was tired of all but death;
So weary was he of his inn,
So sick of being kept within.
If these great men would thence have
    fled,
To leave your inn why should you dread?
That inn from which you daily see
Depart your best-loved company.
Great Cæsar cared not at the last
How soon from such an inn he pass'd.
He would not even take the trouble
To guard what seem'd an empty bubble.

" *Yes, take it*," he did seem to say,
" If you so please, and have your way."

Oh ! shame if any later soul
Should not, like him, prefer the goal
To idling longer in his inn
When he can home eternal win !

So, free and gallant more and more,
Pass you on cheerful from that door ;
Careless, like youth itself, and brave,
Old Honour only seek to save,—
Honour, which, with its mighty span,
Includes your debt to God and man,
Esteeming life now here below
As what can nothing great bestow.
Cheerful, in you let gladness shine ;
But let true courage still be thine—
That spirit, heedless of its skin,
Which deems its body but an inn,
Forwards to press, and reach the land
Where all things you will understand,
Where Love, howe'er divided here,
There, all in One, will have no tear—
At home at last ; your own countree
Will welcome you with heavenly glee ;
Each, of great God the humble guest,
Enjoying everlasting rest.

THE FINALE.

WHEN first we came to the garden fair,
We said, "There's a change, we know not
    where,
In what surrounds us—an alter'd tone,
Nothing defined—'twas by instinct known."
Late in the summer, too late I grant,
Hither we roam'd to see Nature prankt.
Such wild oats as ours, if they're to thrive,
Should be all sown when swallows arrive,
And we should take them out of the ground
When the poor grasshoppers hoarse are found.

Four weeks have pass'd, and we now can trace
The work of Time on poor Nature's face.
Some flowers still raise their bending head,
But the ground is strewn with flow'rets dead.
Red tints grow brown, and the yellow pale;
Each trembling leaf has its winter's tale.
Cold rain in the night has chill'd the air;
The shrubs and flowers seem all less fair;
Insects pugnacious crawl o'er the ground,
Just as shortly will critics be found,

Black, and moreover with turn'd-up tails—
Do let me jest with them ; mirth prevails—
Somebody's coach-horses children call
These spiteful, high-crested things that crawl,
Causing a fright that is quite spasmodic,
And, as the summer ends, periodic ;
Your errant, passant, and rampant devils,
While each your Hill of the Muses levels ;
Angels, sooth, of diminutive race,
Squadrons of smaller with them keep pace ;
Angels that come in leonine form,
All that we love to tear and deform.
Fifty white cocks we might call to aid ;
Not one such devil is frighten'd made ;
Not one will vanish whate'er you show ;
Grubs will still feed where your fresh things
    grow.
On Wordsworth, Byron, and Keats they fed,
So bent on the last they left him dead.
Coming as insects, we must give way ;
Nought we can do will scare them away ;
Looking quite fair, with gossamer wing
Flowers caressing, deeper to sting ;

Who bite while they laugh, laugh while they
    bite,
Leaving their slime on all that's in sight ;
Who feed while vibrating wings in air,
Not like the eagles, that seek their lair

When they have kill'd what they would de-
    vour;
While these glut on wing and need no bower—
These live on wind, eat, drink it as well,
Having for houses vanes, where they dwell;
Merits of different winds their talk,
When on Parnassus they wish to stalk,
The poor Muse's Hill seeming to be
Rome's seven hills that they ever see.
Them you have heard; understand you all,
What critical sleight-of-hand I call?
The Doctor is Scotine, dark, obscure.
Think you his sentences will endure?
Yes; just select now him whom you choose,
Will they outlast a new pair of shoes?
He is antique, laconical, grave,
Concealing his wrath, the more to rave
In the deep ventricles of his brain,
Arterial labyrinth, dubious, vain.
The beans may flower, but he won't fear;
The world to him does wiser appear.
Though it might not be easy to say
In what the modern wisdom lay,
In what lay the folly, past and old,
Which we are warn'd to shun and scold?
What good we draw from the wisdom new,
From folly like that what harm we drew.
Vague words, mere words, much weakness can
    hide,
And pretexts conceal what boils inside;

The cauldron, methinks, is worth the lid,
With which all its black contents are hid.
By the mane you take lions stern, bold,
Buffaloes by the snout you may hold,
Oxen by horns, and wolves by the tail,
Goats by the beard, and birds by the nail
Or claw; but critics you can't restrain
By any bright words; for all they stain.
He who no white can show in his eye [1],
Seems to impel some all to decry.
Imperious, rigorous, grave, and hard,
Inflexible still, they scorn the Bard.
Nothing each believes, nothing he hears,
You can't persuade him by smiles or tears;
So many *ifs* and *buts* he retails,
That e'en of his praise nothing avails.
Does he, I ask, e'en know his own will?
The principal point will lie there still;
The rest depends on whims of the hour,
Just as his temper will smile or lour.
Disjunctives for him are all arms bright,
With which he brandishes doubtful light;
For one part then must ever be true
When he prognosticates all to you.
Bottler of things for which no one cares,
Rusty old measures his only wares,
Proud of his knowledge, he draws it mild,
Hating those venturesome, careless, wild;

[1] The ancients by this term denoted Satan.

Deeply determined, clothed with finesse,
Hiding his spite with that fashion'd dress;
But finesse discover'd, understood,
Loses its finesse, loses its hood,
Loses its essence, even its name;
We call it heaviness, merely shame.
Trust not people who look through a hole;
For things transcendant, they have no soul.

Well, homewards, not sad, we take our way,
Still led by Hope, still playful and gay,
Limp on limb Œdipodic, to climb
Anti-Parnassus, cheer'd with our rhyme,
Feeding on Fancy, toying with verse,
While rolls majestic the universe.

Let the winter come and let leaves fall,
We have yet spirits to bear it all.
Let gusty winds rise, their fury spend,
All that we ask is a faithful friend.
Let critics peep and creep to our side,
For them and for us the world is wide.
Genius of old would let them all fly
Like insects, crawl on the ground and lie.
Why should they not have profit or play,
Short for us both in our common day?
For our final song they yield us wings,
Soaring far off from their angry stings;
But darts like these innocuous fall
On those whose feathers can brave them all.

A a 2

Not one plume would I pluck from their wing,
Nor in their poor breast imprint a sting;
I crave but leave, in my turn, to play,
When I conceive that from truth they stray;
Resentment is silly, yea, unjust;
To fury no one should ever trust.
And what should we do, if sulky grown,
But our sheer folly and weakness own?
Bees leave their life in wounds that they
    make;
Why should we die for Resentment's sake,
Feeding on anger without control—
Anger which is but death to the soul?
Let them cry still, "To perception dull,
We want the sense of the beautiful."
What happier words could reach our ear?
What should less cause us regret or fear?
For if these quick gleams of lustrous
    thought—
These vistas that still abound unsought—
Yielding such glimpses of wild and grand,
Comprising all that is soft and bland,
With shades of bright colour infinite,
And radiant from depths to farthest height,
Combine with my fancy at a glance
To light up my mind, my heart entrance,
As if I beheld those isles of gold,
Gleaming ethereal to snow-tops cold,
Through floods of light o'er the ocean shed,
Paving the path to the sun's bright bed,—

If this be only dulness to cull,
Oh! what must be then the beautiful?
Reveal'd all to them with glad amaze
In their full magic of silent gaze?
To them I owe thanks, not rancour's spite,
For cheering my hopes beyond my might.
Exact information—that's the thing
Each poet needs as well as a king.
No one for giving advice should rue;
Since one man advised is well worth two.
I through my darkness will gladly stray,
And merrily wait for dawn of day.
" Long live field thistles," the donkey cried,
When with the horse he had vainly vied.
Plato declares that a dog is wise;
To get what is scorn'd he always tries.
With what devotion he sees a bone!
With what great care he makes it his own!
With what fervour he holds it in paws!
With what affection its marrow draws!
Well might critics then imitate him,
Not so to flout, and over things skim.
From slippers or socks, a shoe or pad,
What harm to learn, though all from a lad?
Beasts of Arcadia have still a voice
Which can all but the critics rejoice.
Those blest bipeds may sing for the rest;
Some what is branded by them think best.
We are not clerks, to fix on the moon
Our teeth, or drink it with silver spoon.

Though our swallow is never too small,
Sipping, dissolving, deriding all.
Canorous young dogs will think quite sweet
What boys, like thrushes, pipe in the street.
I with such errand-lads meant to sing,
Flapping, like linnets, a merry wing.
Sitting and resting, old sages say,
Proves both the gayest and wisest way.
Feeling we rest, at least to our eyes,
Each day we grow prodigiously wise.

The Muses with Love will still consort ;
That is the sole world in which they sport.
Now Love has but signs, and nothing more,
Mere winks and looks, and of words no store.
But then winks and looks are far more strong
Than the sounds which to talkers belong.
Quite dear to Love they ever avail,
Where all your mere words are counted stale.
Foolish their signs—like sages they rave,
As full of fine folly, mirthful, brave,
As were the deep thoughts of wise men past,
Whose glimpses and visions ever last.

Then, critics, play on, censure and snub ;
Move I will my Diogenic tub.
They say that we dream ; they can't discern
Any thing real that they should learn
From one so constant to fancies old,
Popular, natural, careless, bold.

What are dreams that they seem to despise?
In them a sweet little secret lies.
When sleeping children are put to bed,
Nurses know well no more need be said;
They leave them then, and their pleasures find;
Them to cradles there's nothing to bind.
In this way our souls, when bodies sleep,
Fly to their country, visions to reap.   .
Heaven's our country, and thither we fly,
Wing'd with a dream or a plaintive sigh;
And if *our* dreams but vagueness appear,
Still they descend from our country dear,
Where there are mansions for high and low,
And where, for us all, will sweetness flow.
Let critics expand a broader wing;
Still we mount upwards, like larks, to sing. .
All that we ask is a constant friend,
With whom we can wander, efforts spend;
To catch but a glimpse of what they see—
For us but looming mysteriously.

Then to our Muse will winter be dear;
Mind will see what to eyes can't appear.
Though winds of autumn will fade away,
Through the frore cold air you still can stray.
Morning will have its own freshness glad;
Afternoon walks will never be sad.
While bright are still the regions of air,
'Midst clouds and beams you can saunter there;

Or if on ground you prefer to stay,
The angel guardians met on your way
Salute with constant and cautious care,
Lest you should cause those they tend to stare.
" *Parties* " you call them; the phrase is right—
Each has a comrade, though not in sight.
Love finds wisdom in popular things;
That custom will to your heart give wings.
Bless all in secret those whom you see;
With unseen comrades bid them agree.
The leafless time has its branches high,
Which still point upwards all to the sky.
Your " *hopeless weakness,*" as critics say,
Will frolic and sing, exult all day;
Will mount with its wings tiny and light,
And soar to regions beyond their sight.
They will not mount with it, but deny
That it can float embathed in the sky.
But " weakness " still will triumph to see
How it can bear you mysteriously.
Then, when the dusk reminds you of home,
Thither how gay, how grateful you roam!
Each to his eachdom must repair,
In French, *chascun en chascunière.*
Gladsome we feel; let us welcome Folly,
And banish all angry melancholy.
Let glasses be rinsed, the best be brought,
Let dogs lie down, and the cloth be sought;
Spread it, and serve up, and say no more;
Blow brighter the fire, and shut the door.

Light the candle; and then, while you bask,
Give to the poor whatever they ask.
Watch chesnuts roasting on the bar bright,
Or on the ashes with a stick write;
Hear some fine old tales; tell them in turn;
Believe what you hear, and nothing spurn.
Have you not heard wise Solomon say,
Good men to tales will never say nay?
They believe what you tell, or what you write;
The innocent think that all is right.

But if friends fail, and we're left alone,
Oh! then we shall echo Nature's tone.
O'er the pale leaves of the summer's bier
One of the million then falls your tear.
Fountains of animal spirits dry,
All that is left is to weep and sigh.
The grass that once waved its tresses green,
Fronting the bower of living sheen,
No more will offer a couch and rest,
Golden with soft wind breathed from the West;
But dark, and spotted with faded leaves,
And each foul thing that the ground receives,
Leave it you will to wither and die,
To sounds of the wind that rages nigh.
The rains and the frosts, the fogs and snow,
Will soon cover all that there did grow.
Without is a loneliness, stern, cold,
Within a feeling cannot be told.

Thoughts in which Pleasure can find no room,
Spectral and pale, like ghosts from the tomb.
Hellebore black is what winter knows;
But who can paint what within you grows?

When Spring comes back with its healing wing,
It is not for you the Muses sing.
The charms of life with your friends all fled,
You wait still below; no more is said.
And yet so fondly will Nature cling
To joy, though writhing from mortal sting,
That it will often blindly mistake,
And the long past for the present take.
Seeking insatiably things unknown,
Catching for instants its former tone,
Or fiercely repulsing sense and thought,
As if what is gone could still be sought;
Like Cadenham oak at Christmas-tide,
Which shows a few leaves on ev'ry side;
Or when, as elsewhere, each old oak-tree
Shows by branches how grand it can be.
So once a month, when the skies are clear,
And all lovely hues again appear,
It will entice them wand'ring to stray,
To see those laughing who gaily play,
Singing, dancing, or rolling on grass,
Watching the sparrows that hop and pass;
Spending a day without books, or dread
Of what by others may then be said;

As it were stretching to touch the hem
Of a gay bright dress once worn by them;
Not profitless either, moments few
In which some strength they seem to renew.
Genius, like Love, will seek a pretence,
Come what will, that it may recommence.
So songs and Love with sun-shine return;
The bright piercing spark revives to burn;
They try their poor wings, all closed so long;
Venture to warble a once prized song;
Like swans, that singing will pass the sea[2],
They seek to lighten their misery.
They stretch out their wings, they mount, they
    soar
Away, and are seen and heard no more.

So in this poor world they had their ease,
For truth and goodness them ever please;
Perhaps, still more, they'll find in the next,
Where truth and goodness are never vex'd.
For if they had peace with God and men,
Who can describe what awaits them then?

[2] διαιροῦσι δὲ καὶ τὸ πέλαγος ᾄδοντες. Athen. lib. ix.

LONDON :
GILBERT AND RIVINGTON, PRINTERS.
ST. JOHN'S SQUARE.

www.ingramcontent.com/pod-product-compliance
Lightning Source LLC
Chambersburg PA
CBHW030911270326
41929CB00008B/655